BIRDWATCHING WALKS AROUND MORECAMBE BAY

Birdwatching Walks Around Morecambe Bay

John Wilson BEM Msc and David Hindle MA

Foreword by Joan Morecambe

Artwork by Christine Dodding and Nicola Breaks.
Maps by Christine Dodding.
Colour photographs by Stan Craig ARPS and David Mower.

Colour reference section funded by Arnside/Silverdale AONB

Palatine Books

Copyright © John Wilson and David Hindle, 2007

First published in the UK in 2007 by
Palatine Books
an imprint of Carnegie Publishing Ltd,
Carnegie House,
Chatsworth Road,
Lancaster LA1 4SL
www.palatinebooks.com

Cataloguing-in-Publication data
A catalogue record for this book is available from the British Library

ISBN 1-874181-37-3
EAN 978-1-874181-37-8

Typeset by Carnegie Book Production, Lancaster
Printed and bound in the UK by Cromwell Press, Trowbridge, Wilts

Contents

Foreword

A S A BOY ERIC LOVED THE COUNTRYSIDE and always took a keen interest in identifying and feeding the birds in and around his native Morecambe. In later years it became necessary for the sake of his health to take regular walks, which were made far more interesting by combining them with bird watching, and he could always be seen with his binoculars at the ready. It is no surprise, therefore, that the wonderful statue of Eric (in familiar pose!) which adorns Morecambe promenade also sports a pair of binoculars.

How thrilled he would have been at having a lagoon and hide named after him at the Leighton Moss and Morecambe Bay RSPB Nature Reserve. We, his family, are delighted that the lagoon has proved such a success, especially now that avocets – the emblem of the RSPB, which he supported for many years – have taken to nesting there.

I am also delighted to have been asked to write this foreword to *Birdwatching Walks Around Morecambe Bay*. As Eric knew very well, the area is rich in bird life and there are many beautiful walks during which they can be seen. It is a combination which I know he would have enjoyed and I am sure that it will prove to be very popular with walkers and birdwatchers from both near and far.

Joan Morecambe
March 2007

Introduction and authors' preface

THE MORECAMBE BAY AREA is one of the finest bird watching sites in Britain. Centred on the 310 square kilometres of inter-tidal sand flats it is an outstanding combination of habitats – off shore islands, sand dunes, rocky shore, salt marsh, brackish lagoon, reed-bed, open water, woodland, scrub, grassland, river valleys, farmland and heather moorland. All this set against a backdrop of the Lakeland, Pennine and Bowland fells. The bay itself, a complex of five rivers – the Wyre, Lune, Keer, Kent and Leven – is designated a Special Protection Area under the European Birds Directive. There is a host of other protected areas around the bay, which includes Sites of Special Scientific Interest, Ramsar Sites and Nature Reserves, run by several different organisations, including English Nature, RSPB and the Lancashire and Cumbria Wildlife Trusts. The Arnside/Silverdale and Bowland areas are both designated as Areas of Outstanding Natural Beauty, all testifying to the richness and importance of the area for wildlife.

This book, with forty specially chosen walks, covers Morecambe Bay, from the Wyre estuary in the south to Walney Island in the north, embraces the neighbouring Duddon estuary and the peripheral areas of the southern Lake District and Forest of Bowland. It describes where and when to find the birds and other wildlife in this unique area.

However, before setting out to watch and enjoy the birds of the area, there are certain important points that *must* be considered.

Tides

For safety reasons – and to get the most out of each walk – it is imperative to consult the tide tables before setting out on any of the walks along the coast. To help those with little or no knowledge about tides to understand the need for such precautions, a simple, brief explanation of tidal cycles may help. The life-blood of an estuary is the tide which, twice daily, covers the sands with nutrient-rich waters. The tidal height changes each day – basically seven days of low tides, called neap tides, are followed by seven days of higher tides, rather confusingly called spring tides. Overlaying this roughly two-week cycle is an annual cycle where the highest tides occur close to the spring and autumnal equinoxes. Remember also that the tide goes out the furthest on the higher tides, so exposing more feeding grounds for the birds.

Tides are caused by the gravitational pull of the sun, and more especially, the moon, with the highest tides occurring at full and new moon. It is important to remember though that tide height can be seriously affected by strong on-shore winds. Under extreme conditions a rise of a metre or so is not uncommon and if this happens at the same time as a high spring tide, the sea defences can be over topped, car parks flooded and serious damage caused. Conversely, strong off-shore winds can result in lower tides than predicted.

Tidal heights referred to are for the Liverpool tide tables, though tide tables are also published for Fleetwood, Morecambe, and Barrow. Tide times vary within the bay itself, with high tide being 5–8 minutes later on the north and west of the bay than the east. The higher, or spring tides, always occur around mid-day, ideal for bird watching on a short winter's day.

The daily routine of wading birds is based around the tidal cycle rather than that of day and night. When the tide is out and the sand flats are exposed the waders feed on the abundant invertebrates. There are, however, marked differences between species, depending on where the invertebrates that each species specializes on are located. Oystercatchers, for example, feed mainly on mussels and cockles, which occur on the lower and middle shore, the area last to be exposed and first to be covered by the tide. In contrast, Dunlin and Redshank feed a great deal on sand hoppers, which occur in the middle and upper shores, so these species have a longer period to search for their prey. However, in mid-winter, when the spring tide is around mid-day, many species will have a maximum of only 4 to 5 hours to feed. This is not long enough to sustain them so they also feed at low water during the night. Convincing evidence that they are awake and active is the almost constant chorus of oystercatchers audible from Morecambe promenade at low water during the hours of darkness.

With the flowing of the tide each species stops feeding when their preferred feeding grounds are covered and they make their way to the high tide roost site, which, on neap tides, will often be on an exposed sand bank, or, on spring tides, on the salt marshes or shingle beaches. On extreme spring tides when even these refuges are covered, they resort to fields just behind the sea wall. Over the high tide period, most species rest, often standing on one leg with the bill tucked under the scapular feathers. However, they quickly take to the wing if any danger threatens.

High tide is also the best time to observe flocks of wildfowl as they float in with the incoming tide. Many ducks feed inland after dark but spend the day roosting on the inter-tidal area. Conversely, geese feed inland during the day but fly to the marshes and sand flats to roost at night.

Most coastal walks are best undertaken on spring tides and on each of the following walks the best tide heights are indicated, together with some idea of the time to start the walk in relation to the time of high tide, so maximising the possibility of successful bird watching.

Timing

Because of the abundance of birds on many walks, the timing is considerably longer than it would take to simply walk the route. On a high tide wader roost, for example, the suggested time allows you both to watch the flocks assemble then to scan through the many thousands of roosting birds. Both will involve periods of just standing, especially if you take the recommended good telescope. One of the attractions of bird watching is the element of unpredictability. Visiting a site like Leighton Moss does not guarantee a sighting of a bittern or a bearded tit but the longer you stop in a hide the better the odds. And what a thrill it is when one appears so again, this has been allowed for in the timings given. Remember also that species described on the walks have to be searched for, which again takes time.

The time of year is, of course, also important. Coastal waders and wildfowl are largely present from late July to late May. The period March to June is the prime time for resident breeding birds, with late April to June the optimum period for summer migrants.

Distance

The distances given are an indication of the length of a direct walk. In practice, when bird watching you often deviate from the path to check a sighting and, on occasions, re-trace your steps if something special turns up, so the distances should be treated as an approximate guide.

Bird numbers and feeding habits

In the short accounts accompanying the photographs we have attempted to give some idea of the bay's population for most of the wintering wildfowl and waders. The figure given is the five-year average peak count based on the Wetland Bird Survey (WeBS), which is jointly organised by the British Trust for Ornithology and the Wildfowl and Wetlands Trust. The count is undertaken each month, not only on Morecambe Bay but throughout Britain, by a large team of dedicated observers.

While on the subject of bird numbers, a summary of why there are so many waders and wildfowl on the estuary may be of interest. Naturally, the main reason is the abundance of invertebrates living in the sand and mud of an estuary. Bivalves are the most abundant, ranging from the delicate pink Baltic telling, with maximum density of over 50,000 per square metre, to the larger and more well known mussels and cockles, which are found in dense beds. These have densities sometimes as high as 200,000 per square metre when very small,(or spat as the young cockles and mussels are called) and are taken especially by knot and dunlin and when larger by oystercatchers. The small sandhopper *corophium* lives in U-shaped burrows often along creeks, attains densities of 9000 per square metre and is taken especially by dunlin and redshank. The tiny snail *hydrobia* can reach densities of 10,000 per square metre, is found on the middle and upper shore and is taken by ringed plover and shelduck. All these abundant invertebrates live in the top two to five centimetres of the sand.

Two marine worms, the lug and rag worms, live much deeper in the sand and are available only to the long-billed curlew and godwits, and they occur at much lower densities, usually under 100 per square metre.

Details of the amazing migration that birds undertake are also given, mainly based on recoveries of ringed birds. Locally this is based on the work of the two ringing groups covering the bay area for waders: the Morecambe Bay Ringing Group and for other species, the North Lancashire Ringing Group. Details of these can be found on the Lancaster Bird Watching website as detailed below.

Maps

A sketch map is provided with each walk to guide the visitor through the recommended route. These are only rough guides, however, and should be used in conjunction with Landranger Maps 96, 97, 102, which cover the area described.

Facilities for disabled

Bird watching by wheelchair and mobility buggy is becoming more popular. To encourage this further, where appropriate wheelchair access is indicated by the disabled symbol. On many walks there is only partial disabled access and this is briefly described at the start of the walk. However, on most walks good bird watching may be enjoyed at selected locations from the comfort of a car.

Further information

Up-to-date information can be found by visiting the following websites:

www.fyldebirdclub.org.uk for the Fylde to Lune estuary and inland
www.lancasterbirdwatching.org.uk for the area from the Lune to the Kent and inland
www.cumbriabirdclub.org.uk for Cumbria
www.eastlancsornithologists.org.uk

Further reading

Birds of Lancashire and North Merseyside, White, 2007
Birds of Lancashire, Oakes, 1953
Birds of Morecambe Bay, Wilson, 1988
The Status and distribution of Birds in Lancashire, Spencer, 1975
The Atlas of Breeding Birds of Lancashire and North Merseyside, Pyfinch and Goulbourn, 2001
The Breeding Birds of Cumbria, Stott et al., 2002
Birdwatching Walks in Cumbria, Dean and Roberts, 2002
Birdwatching Walks in Bowland, Hindle and Wilson, 2005

Four bird reports are published annually covering different parts of the area: the Lancashire Bird Report, the Cumbria Bird Report, the Fylde Bird Report and the Lancaster and District Bird Report. Details of these can be found on the above websites.

The country code

Naturally the country code should be strictly observed, namely – drop no litter, close all gates, do not damage walls or fences, or in any way disturb stock, avoid all fire risks, and *remember* it is now unlawful to dig up or pick many species of wildflowers. You should also avoid unnecessary disturbance of roosting waders and wildfowl.

- Be safe – plan ahead and follow any signs
- Leave gates and property as you find them
- Protect plants and animals and take your litter home
- Keep your dog under close control
- Consider other people

A safety warning

- Always consult the tide tables before setting out
- Beware of rapidly advancing tides and quicksand. Do not wander out onto the inter-tidal area or away from paths on the salt marshes
- Take special care on extreme wind-driven high tides under such conditions
- Some car parking sites mentioned in this book can be flooded

Disclaimer

The authors have walked and researched the routes for the purposes of this guide. Whilst every effort has been made to represent the routes accurately, neither the authors nor the publisher can accept any responsibility in connection with any trespass, loss of injury arising from the route of the definitive route or any associated route. Changes may occur in the landscape, which may affect the information in this book and the authors and publisher would very much welcome notification of any such changes. That said, we sincerely hope that the walks provide many hours of enjoyable bird watching.

Acknowledgements

ONCE again it is a pleasure to acknowledge the help given by the following people and organisations in the production of this book. Joan Morecambe for kindly writing the forward. Barbara Craig for supplying the excellent photographs taken by her late husband Stan Craig, ARPS. David Mower for his outstanding photographs. Christine Dodding and Nicola Breaks for their artistry. Garth Sutcliffe for reading and commenting on the final draft, and all our friends and bird watching acquaintances for supplying information and sightings.

Oystercatcher

An ornithological treasure trail: from Fleetwood to Rossall hospital

(may be extended to Blackpool)

Leaches petrol

Start: Start and finish at Fleetwood Pier
Grid reference: SD335485
Distance: 11 km (6.8 miles)
Time: 4 to 5 hours (Rossall Hospital)
Grade: Easy
General: Tourist Information, car parking, toilet and
refreshment facilities at Fleetwood
♿ Fleetwood Promenade is suitable for
wheelchairs

THE LENGTH OF BEACH between Fleetwood and Rossall Hospital provides excellent opportunities for birding. Bird watching is, however, often tide and weather dependent and it should be remembered that a fine day in summer will yield quite a pleasant walk but not necessarily many birds. You are recommended to commence the walk about two hours before high water on tides above 8.5 metres, allowing time to absorb the fabulous views of Morecambe Bay, which broadly equate to the geographical area covered by this book. While enjoying a cup of best flask coffee or stewed tea, you may even be inspired to select your next walk from the vista before you, while reflecting on the birding potential across the Wyre estuary at Knott End and Over Wyre, or north towards the Bowland Hills, Sunderland Point and the estuaries of the Lune, Kent, Leven and Duddon, flanked by the hills and mountains of southern Lakeland. On a clear day, the white edifice of Barrow's Walney Lighthouse betrays the location of the Furness Peninsula and the shipyards of Barrow, all overshadowed by the distinctive isolated shape of Black Combe, fringeing Cumbria's coastline to the north of Millom.

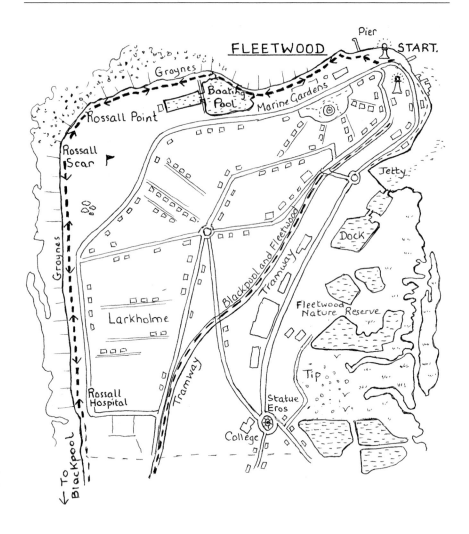

The development of the fishing town and coastal holiday resort of Fleetwood owes its existence to wealthy philanthropist Peter Hesketh Fleetwood, who persuaded renowned architect, Decimus Burton, to design an accessible holiday resort. The coming of the railway in 1840 led to Victorian expansion of Fleetwood, both as a holiday resort and as a port that developed to become home to the third largest fleet of trawlers in the country. Fleetwood is still an attractive resort with much of its Victorian origins still evident. For some strange reason one of the town's two light-houses, Pharoe's, is situated in the middle of the main shopping street. I see no ships – only tramcars! Adding to the period charm is the sight and sound of Blackpool's unique tramcars, regularly clanking along twin tracks in the middle of the high street, just as they have done for over a century.

Landward is Fleetwood's only raised area, 'The Mount'. On reaching the summit – definitely not for the faint-hearted – dispense with those crampons and take a well-earned break!

1. *Commence walking south from Fleetwood's Victorian pier along the promenade to the Floral Hall. An optional ascent of The Mount may be attempted, before regaining the promenade and Fleetwood boating lake. Continue to walk the esplanade with the sea on one side and a golf course on the other. Pass the disused coastguard station before eventually reaching Rossall Hospital. Here there are two options – retrace your steps along the same route or extend your walk to Cleveleys and Blackpool, returning by tramcar to Fleetwood Pier.*

The early bird catches the worm, according to the old saying, and diurnal passage migration along the coast may be observed from first light to mid-morning. At Fleetwood, records typically include flocks of pied wagtail, grey wagtail, meadow pipit, chaffinch, starling, goldfinch, siskin and less common species, such as yellow wagtail and tree pipit. Good winter passerine sightings have included snow bunting, twite and the occasional black redstart and rock pipit, which should be looked for anywhere along the shore line or, inland of the sea wall, on the grassy areas and waste land between the golf course and Rossall Hospital.

Weather permitting it is possible to witness seasonal migration at the mount. The wooded plantation of sycamore, pine and hawthorn, situated in a sheltered hollow at the rear of the building has been known to attract migrant passerines with sightings of pied and spotted flycatcher and there are September records of icterine and yellow browed warbler. The complexities of little brown jobs, colloquially known as LBJs, can be both frustrating and difficult – so have the bird book handy, just in case! However, this is hardly an east coast bird observatory with regular falls of migrants, and usually the bird scene might best be described as 'rather quiet', so just relax and enjoy the view.

Fleetwood foreshore has had its share of wintering white winged gulls, (glaucous and Iceland and Mediterranean gull). An exceptionally rare winter visitor from the arctic, a Ross's Gull, was found close to Fleetwood boating pool in January, 1965. This serves to illustrate that when birding, anything can turn up and almost everything that moves, including the more usual flocks of black headed, common, herring, lesser and greater black-backed gulls should be scrutinised.

At Fleetwood boating lake cormorant, goldeneye and red-breasted merganser often join large flocks of mute swans and, on the island, turnstone and redshank may be seen roosting at high tide. Indeed, wader flocks may be seen to good advantage throughout this walk but especially between the boating lake and Rossall Point. At high tide in winter, redshank, oystercatcher, ringed plover, turnstone and sanderling roost on the mud and pebbles and feed further out on the estuarine mudflats when the tide recedes. Sightings of the occasional purple sandpiper are not without precedent and today's ringed plovers tread in the footsteps of one of their most revered relatives, the Kentish plover, very rare on Lancashire's west coast. A single bird was present at Rossall Point for five consecutive winters between 1992 and 1997, incredibly always returning on or about the 20th November and departing to its mysterious summer haunt in early March. The bird was last recorded on the 9th March 1997.

Scan the golf course from the promenade where stonechat seem to be quite at home and wheatears may typically be seen in late March with characteristic upright stance and distinctive plumage, heralding the arrival of spring. Golf courses occasionally turn up rarities that have included here tawny pipit and an American golden plover, so take a close look at any likely suspects without upsetting the golfers! Botanical interest along the promenade and at the edges of the golf course includes sea holly and the attractive sea bindweed; the flora attracts large colourful butterflies like small tortoiseshell, red admiral, peacock, painted lady and that rare migrant butterfly, the clouded yellow.

The now defunct coastguard station is an excellent spot for a sea watch. Wintering eider duck at Rossall Point have reached flocks up to 1,000, feeding over the mussel beds with smaller numbers of common scoter, cormorant and great crested grebe. In winter, red-throated diver should easily be seen, whereas in spring there is a more pronounced passage, with occasional records of both great northern and black-throated diver. There is also evidence of the exciting and uncommon pomarine skua appearing as a passage migrant during April and May.

On return passage during late summer and autumn, Arctic skuas harass offshore flocks of sandwich, common, Arctic and little tern. All three species of skua, great, pomarine and long tailed, have been recorded, and exceptionally rare seabirds sighted offshore over the years have included sabines gull, sooty shearwater and cory's shearwater.

Seasonal storms have contributed to sightings of storm petrel, gannet, kittiwake, fulmar, Manx shearwater, razorbill, guillemot and rare sightings of black guillemot. Timing and weather conditions are crucial in attempting to see one of Lancashire's specialities, the Leach's petrel which should be looked for between September and early December between Rossall and Blackpool. Perhaps the ideal time to be propping up the sea wall is when Blackpool illuminations have taken a battering the night before from sustained westerly or south-westerly gale-force winds.

The quest for such ornithological treasures is really what birding is all about and finding one provides a time to reflect on this truly oceanic, nomadic wanderer of the North Atlantic Ocean. One may contemplate the origins of Leach's petrel and whether it will make it to some mysterious destination. Unfortunately, on reaching alien coastal waters in the shadow of Blackpool Tower, the tired birds are sometimes predated by a reception committee of opportunistic gulls.

Such sitings make a refreshing and breezy change from the image of Blackpool, with its fish and chips, tramcars and other nostalgic memories of the flamboyant resort during the 20th Century. From the North Pier during autumn, it is possible to watch Leach's petrel but doubtless they will not share the same feeling of well-being in the midst of a force eight or nine. Hopefully, they will return to traditional haunts for many years to come.

Meadow pipit

N.B.

The Wyre experience

Black Tailed Godwit.

Start: Start and finish at Stanah Wyre-side Ecology Centre

Grid reference: SD 355431

Distance: Each of two walks is about 10.5 km (6.5 miles)

Time: Each is between 4 and 5 hours

Grade: Easy

General: Tourist Information, toilet, refreshment and car parking facilities at Stanah

♿ Wheelchair access from Stanah to view river and marsh

Walk 2A

THESE TWO EASY WALKS, beginning and ending at Stanah Wyreside Ecology Centre, offer alternative north or south walks along the south bank of the Wyre and within the country park. Alternatively, a return combined walk is offered. Distances are left to the discretion of the walker but it is suggested that the limits are Shard Bridge (south) and Fleetwood Marsh (north). You need to be aware that at high tide the paths along the river bank may be flooded and it may be dangerous to venture onto the salt marsh or mudflats. Tidal information is available from the centre, where Countryside Rangers promote conservation, maintain public rights of way and lead guided walks. To contact a Ranger or find out about facilities, either visit the Ecology Centre or telephone on 01253 857890.

The Wyre estuary forms the southern boundary of Morecambe Bay and is significant in international terms for its populations of pink-footed geese, teal, black-tailed godwit and redshank. The River Wyre is 52 kilometres long from its source to the sea, and is the third largest river in Lancashire after the Ribble and the Lune. The Wyre Estuary Country Park includes the whole estuary from Fleetwood and Knott End up river as far as Shard Bridge. The riverside path offers excellent views over the estuary, which may also be enjoyed from the bird hide situated to the north of the ecology centre and from where the key may be obtained.

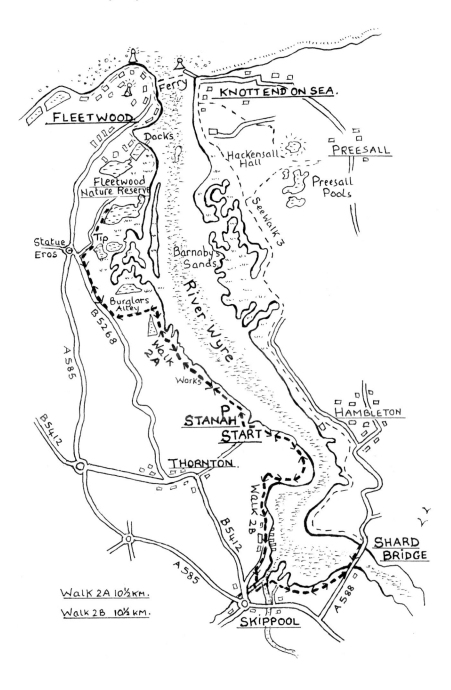

Walk 2A 10½ km.

Walk 2B 10½ km.

1. *Leave the Wyre Ecology Centre and follow the riverside path northwards, past the bird hide and alongside the I.C.I. works to its northern boundary. Gain the uncompromisingly named Burglar's Alley by walking left between two high iron fences and crossing over a disused mineral line to Fleetwood Road. The walk from Burglar's Alley, via Jameson Road, to Fleetwood Marsh reserve (indicated on the map) is prolonged and urbanised so most people prefer to drive to Fleetwood Marsh. It is accessed by a minor road close to the junction of the A585 and B5268.*

Flocks of knot, dunlin and sanderling prevail nearer the mouth of the estuary, where typically common tern, sandwich tern, cormorant, eider and commoner species of gull may be observed. Grey herons are plentiful throughout the area and that other recent colonist from Mediterranean climes, the little egret, is increasingly becoming established in northern England and should now be sought on the mudflats and marshes.

Wader and wildfowl populations are based on seasonal change, thus stimulating interest throughout the year. In winter, large flocks of lapwing, golden plover, black-tailed godwit, ringed plover, curlew and redshank feed on the mudflats along the estuary and upriver to Shard Bridge. They are joined by flocks of wildfowl and large numbers of pink-footed geese and teal, which often roost on Barnaby's Sands and Burrows' Marsh on the north bank, opposite the I.C.I Works, with smaller numbers of mallard, wigeon and shelduck. Flocks of starling, finches and skylarks winter on salt marshes, which in turn attract kestrel, sparrowhawk, merlin and short-eared owl.

In spring there are influxes of dunlin, sanderling and black-tailed godwit migrating north to their northern breeding grounds, while many lapwings, curlew and oyster-catcher return to favourable local breeding grounds such as the Forest of Bowland, generally returning to the estuary around mid July at the commencement of the autumn migration. Wintering species begin to arrive in late September and increase throughout October to November. Snipe and the occasional jack snipe are more at home on the salt marshes and should also be looked for during this period.

Golden Plover

Kingfishers occur as residents on both the salt marsh creeks and freshwater pools. Behind the embankment at the I.C.I. works there are several fresh water lagoons that hold mute swan, great crested and little grebe and occasionally that scarce, spring migrant duck, the garganey. Stoats and foxes represent the mammalian contingent and are often associated with urbanised land. Burglar's Alley is a lengthy, hedgerow-lined walkway leading from the shore to Fleetwood Road, where there is potential for passerine migrants, exemplified by sightings of both redstart and ring ousel. However, you should not raise your expectations too high.

The small Lancashire Wildlife Trust Reserve of 0.5ha comprises fresh water pools and lies in an old railway cutting. Here, the main points of interest are the breeding reed warblers, roosting swallows and its attraction for passage migrants. Water rail and snipe are frequent winter visitors, whilst a summer visit reveals a flourish of flora and fauna, including colonies of marsh orchids and bee orchids and rare dragonflies. A selection of butterflies including common blue, large skipper, red admiral, painted lady, small tortoiseshell, speckled wood, meadow brown and wall brown may be seen both here and throughout the walk to Skippool.

Walk 2B: the Live Wyre

1. *Leave the Wyre Ecology Centre and follow the riverside path south all the way to Skippool and/or Shard Bridge and return via the same route.*

The hedgerows along the river provide nesting and feeding cover for a variety of commoner species, autumn berries attract flocks of Scandinavian redwing and fieldfare and occasional brambling may also be seen around the centre or feeding nearby with chaffinches. Collared doves are resident and in spring whitethroat, willow warbler, garden warbler and sedge warbler are quite common.

August and September welcome many waders migrating to their wintering quarters in West Africa, so this is the best time to see less common species such as whimbrel, curlew sandpiper, little stint, greenshank, spotted redshank and ruff, which can typically be found at low tide on the mudflats between Skippool and Shard Bridge. The latter site is surprisingly good for common sandpipers with flocks of up to thirty recorded. By contrast, vagrant migrants should be closely looked for on the tidal mudflats, especially in the vicinity of Shard Bridge and Skippool, where Lancashire's first great knot was identified by local birdwatcher, Chris Batty, during July, 2004. Clearly, careful scrutiny is required and, like the policeman walking his beat, it is better to be armed with a pen and notebook and to obtain corroborative evidence of all likely suspects. For example, American vagrants have included ringed bill gull and white rumped sandpiper and, for rarities such as these full documentation is required for acceptance.

Skippool has had its share of notoriety as well as rare birds and was originally the old port of Poulton-le-Fylde. Here, in the mid-18th century, ships from Russia and Barbados would unload their cargoes of wine, rum, sugar and tobacco. It was, however, the coming of the railway to Fleetwood in 1840 that led to the demise of Skippool as a port. Thereafter, a policeman walking his beat would no longer have his attention drawn to the local press gangs, ale houses, cock fighting and smuggling activities that were associated with this infamous port. Just like the music hall gag, these activities have been consigned to history – at least we hope so!

Greenshank   CD.

All aboard the 'Pilling Pig' to Knott End on Sea

Start: Start and finish at the main car park close to the jetty, Knott End

Grid reference: SD 347486

Distance: 12 km (7.5 miles)

Time: 4 to 5 hours

Grade: Easy

General: Free parking, refreshment and toilet facilities at Knott End and Preesall

    Wheelchair access at Knott End to view river

THE CONSTRUCTION OF THE GARSTANG, Pilling and Knott End branch line commenced to Pilling in 1870 and was completed through to Knott End in 1908 to link with the Knott End ferry. The line closed to passenger traffic in 1930 and segments of the line closed to freight from 1950. A feature of this walk is that between Preesall and Knott End we birdwatch along the track-bed of the former railway. This was the haunt of a vintage 1875 'Hudswell Clarke' steam engine that was known locally as the 'Pilling Pig' because of the loud shrieking whistle, said by locals to resemble a dying, screaming pig.

It is nice to combine natural history with a modicum of local history, so it is interesting to note that Preesall once boasted a local salt industry with its own salt mines, and it was at Preesall's Black Bull pub that salt was first discovered in 1872. The discovery of vast deposits of rock salt below Preesall led to the founding of a major industry on the banks of the Wyre. The salt was extracted by pumping freshwater in and brine out and a number of old brine wells are still visible. Eventually serious flooding of the brine wells led to their closure in 1930.

The walk passes the 17th-century Hackensall Hall which was largely rebuilt during the late Victorian era for Richard Hesketh-Fleetwood, the founder of

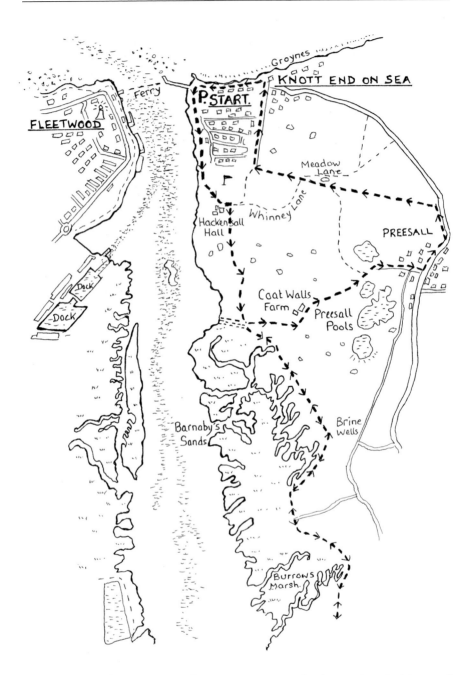

Fleetwood, and incorporates the Wyre estuary and salt marshes. Evidence of ancient settlers can be found in local place names such as Preesall (Celtic) and Hackensall (Norse, named after a Viking settler called Haakon).

1. *From the car park at Knott End on Sea (site of the old railway station) walk the Wyre Way footpath upstream to the fishermen's cottages, turning left in front of Sea Dyke Cottage at the edge of the golf course. Follow the grassy path along the right hand side of the course behind the cottages. Watch out for stray golf balls while heading diagonally left across the course towards a wood and Hackensall Hall. Just beyond Hackensall Hall, turn right along the Wyre Way and continue for one mile to the second junction of paths. To the right is an overgrown grassy track, which is all that remains of the track-bed of a mineral line that linked Preesall salt mines with a jetty on the River Wyre at Arm Hill – circa 1920s. Walk along this bastion of local industrial archaeology to the site of the jetty where rock salt was once loaded onto ships for export to countries as far afield as Canada and India. This is an ideal spot to eat a packed lunch while watching the tide, with clear views of Barnaby's Sands and the river. Retrace your steps to the junction and follow the Wyre Way upstream as far as you want, to view more of Barnaby's Sands and Burrows Marsh.*

For this walk, any time of the year can be productive for birds. If possible, choose to commence walking the first section of the walk along the Wyre Way about three hours before high tide. Knott End on Sea overlooks the Wyre estuary and Fleetwood. On a clear day the view across the bay towards the Lake District mountains of Coniston Old Man and Black Combe is awe-inspiring.

Knott End
Ferry Crossing.

C.Dodding

During the autumn of 2005 a particularly commendable crow, the chough, was a surprising visitor to Knott End golf course and adjacent farmland. Choughs are normally sedentary and the nearest established colonies are on the Isle of Man and at Anglesey; indeed there are very few Lancashire records. The Knott End foreshore and marshes attract flocks of twite in winter, small numbers of snow bunting, and rock pipits – listen for their distinctive calls. Cormorants, eider and great crested grebes commonly pass by on the river. The sands and marshes offer good wader watching, particularly during the high tide roosts when there are often large numbers of oystercatchers, redshanks, lapwing, turnstone, dunlin, ringed plover, golden plover, grey plover, black-tailed and bar-tailed godwits, knot, snipe, common sandpiper and curlew. Greenshank, whimbrel and common terns are both seasonal visitors over river and marsh, whilst curlew sandpiper are occasionally seen on the mudflats in early autumn, with rarer species more usual further upstream nearer to Shard Bridge.

Little terns may occasionally be seen fishing over the estuary but at Arm Hill this species is now unfortunately extinct as a Lancashire breeding bird, although during recent years vegetation has been removed from the shingle in an attempt to attract little terns to nest here again. The Wyre estuary contains the largest area of ungrazed salt marsh in north-west England and is important for wintering waders and wildfowl. The Lancashire Wildlife Trust Reserves of Barnaby's Sands (grid reference SD 355450 – 67ha) and Burrows Marsh (grid reference SD350461 – 36.5ha) are of particular botanical interest. During July three species of sea lavender occur: lax flowered, sea lavender and the rare rock sea lavender. Other plants to look for include sea-blite, sea purslance, sea aster and thrift. The marshes are worth a close inspection for that increasing Mediterranean species, the little egret. Seasonal wildfowl include mallard, wigeon, teal, red-breasted merganser, goldeneye, shelduck and eider. Wintering flocks of pink-footed geese roost on the marshes and mudflats.

2. *Having viewed the marsh, retrace your steps to the junction and proceed along the gravel track indicated by the footpath sign 'Town Foot' (Preesall) 1 mile. The route to Preesall via Coat Walls Farm is straightforward and leads left onto the main street. Pass by (or otherwise!) the Saracen's Head and Black Bull pubs and walk downhill to a rise in the road that marks the site of the former Preesall railway station. Look for a public footpath sign on the left side of the main road and descend several steps to gain the old track-bed, then follow it towards Knott End for about two kilometres across open agricultural land. At a junction of paths, continue straight ahead into more dense cover, emerging by the side of a former level crossing keeper's cottage. At this point the railway tends to run through the middle of someone's house and we turn right along a residential road to emerge in Knott End. Turn left to gain the promenade and quickly pass by the Bourne Arms to the starting point at the old station site, not forgetting to hand in your train ticket!*

Snow Bunting (photo by C. Dodding)

Farming land close to Coat Wall's Farm and Preesall can be very productive and sympathetic farming seems to benefit the birds, including the local swallow population. Typical farmland birds may include stock dove, skylark, reed bunting, chaffinch, linnet, goldfinch, greenfinch, meadow pipit, pied wagtail, house sparrow and the sadly declining tree sparrow. Check the hedges in spring and autumn for whitethroat, sedge warbler, willow warbler and garden warbler. It is also possible to see barn, tawny and little owl hereabouts and occasionally in winter, short-eared owl and hen harrier. Heron, mallard, tufted duck, coot, waterhen and great crested grebe are commonly present on Preesall fishing lakes, together with reed and sedge warblers.

Peregrines, kestrels and sparrow hawks all hunt over the fields and estuary but merlin are less commonly seen. Buzzards may now be seen flying overhead or sometimes perched. They were formally uncommon in many areas of Lancashire up to the 1980s but since then a combination of factors has contributed to expansion. For example, human persecution has decreased with enlightenment and the main prey species, the rabbit, seems to have recovered from the impacts of myxomatosis.

Throughout the walk look out for several species of butterfly, including common blue, speckled wood, red admiral, peacock, small tortoiseshell, large skipper, painted lady, wall, meadow hedge brown and several species of dragonflies. Returning to Knott End, a high tide wader roost often assembles east of Knott End and can be viewed from the shore path towards Fluke Hall.

The Wyre taster

Water Rail. C.D.

Start: Starts and finishes at Scorton picnic centre
Grid reference: 506504
Distance: 1.5 km (0.9 miles)
Time: 1 hour
Grade: Easy
General: Toilet and refreshment facilities at Scorton village
    Wheelchair access at Scorton to view the river

BEFORE COMMENCING EITHER WALK, check the bird feeders at the picnic centre for great spotted woodpecker, chaffinch, siskin, nuthatch and titmice.

1. *From the picnic centre car park, gain the footpath on the east bank of the river and walk the short distance north to a bird hide overlooking a mere. Continue along the path, before veering off right through woodland and returning on a circular walk to the car park.*

Typical birds associated with fast flowing rivers such as this include the dipper and grey wagtail, common sandpiper and kingfisher. Riverine woodlands harbour bullfinch, siskin, jay, several species of titmice, goldcrest and roe deer. In spring listen for willow warblers, blackcaps and garden warblers in the scrub and foliage.

The wren is a surprisingly skilful vocalist and likely to be located moving through the complex maze of ground cover. The intriguing thing about the tiny wren is that the male builds several elaborate domed nests for the female, who selects only one then adds feathers to the lining. The other nests are not always wasted, however, as the crafty polygamous males may

Heron

play away from home and have a different mate in each. By contrast, the harsh rasping sound of jays usually reveal a glance of their colourful plumage flying through the alder thickets, where lesser redpolls and siskins should be looked for, especially during the winter months. At this season too, those Scandinavian thrushes, redwings and fieldfares are active, moving down the valley in loose mixed flocks.

During winter it may be possible to spot the secretive water rail in the aquatic vegetation. Listen out for its distinctive groaning call, rather reminiscent of a pig being strangled – a sort of sudden, explosive onslaught of shrill squeals, diminishing in clarity to a faint terminal flourish.

The pace is relaxed and from the bird hide you can observe the mind-boggling array of species including two coot, moorhen, mute swan, motley mallards and even tufted duck. In the summer time check the surface for 'odanata' – damsel and dragonflies – and feast your eyes upon the superb peacock butterfly gracing the heads of knapweed.

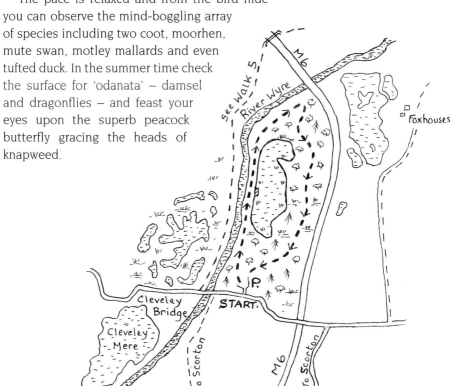

Walking the Wyre:
Scorton to Dolphinholme

Start: Starts and finishes at Scorton picnic centre
Grid reference: 506504
Distance: 9.5 km (5.9 miles)
Time: 4 to 5 hours
Grade: Easy
General: Toilet and refreshment facilities at Scorton village
♿ Wheelchair access at Scorton to view the river

IN EITHER DIRECTION THIS WALK EMBRACES a diverse range of riverine habitats and man made meres, woodlands and woodland edge bordering fields and delightful, quiet country lanes with mature hedgerows, set against a backcloth of the Bowland fells. From the bridge watch the river for dipper, kingfisher, pied and grey wagtail. In spring the liquid calls of common sandpipers flying low over the river usually betray their presence. The bramble-dominated scrub, alder and birch woodland hold common passerines, already described on the first walk.

1. *This circular walk follows the Wyre Way logo on the west side of the river from Scorton picnic centre to Dolphinholme and returns via the east side of the river.*

2. *Scorton to Dolphinholme: from the picnic centre cross over Cleveley road bridge to gain the west bank of the Wyre and follow the Wyre Way north (indicated 'Nan's Nook.) Emerge from the river bank into fields and veer left to cross over a footbridge spanning the M6. After Guy's Farm the Wyre Way reaches Wyresdale Lakes before emerging onto a road at Street Bridge. Cross over the road and follow the Wyre Way to Dolphinholme via Corless Mill*

3. *Dolphinholme to Scorton: at Dolphinholme turn right onto the main street, passing Rivers View Fold, then turn right onto the Wyre circular walk, proceeding through a small conifer wood and fields. Pass the rear of Wyresdale Hall on the right and turn right at a junction to reach the footpath on the left just before Street Bridge. Return to Scorton picnic site, via the hamlet of Foxhouses by following the Wyre circular walk logo.*

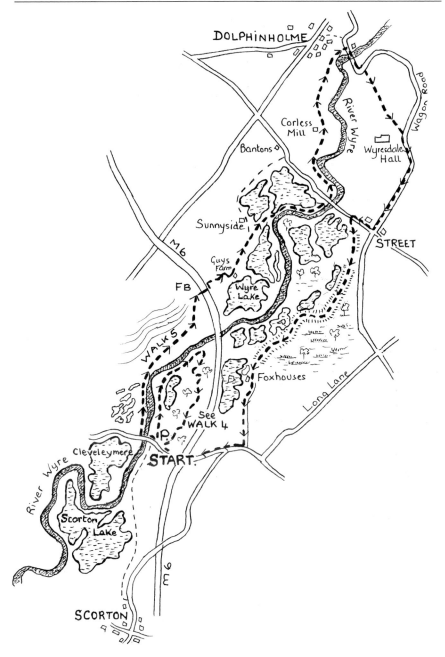

Birds of prey such as kestrel, sparrowhawk, peregrine and buzzard can be expected almost anywhere in this habitat close to Bowland. The buzzard, often known as 'the tourist's eagle', is now officially regarded as the most abundant bird of prey in the U.K. and breeding takes place in most counties. Likewise, the largest member of the crow family, the raven, is now being seen more frequently in peripheral areas of the Forest of Bowland. Recognition of its distinct croaking call flying high above is an important aid to identification, together with its characteristic flight profile. Ravens may be encountered anywhere on this walk.

Former gravel pits at Wyresdale Lakes offering trout and course fishing are a haven for fishermen, offering trout and coarse fishing, and include those avian specialists in the same field, such as goosander and heron. Tufted duck, mute swan, great crested grebe and little grebe all nest here along with moorhen and even the proverbial two coot! A few pairs of common terns have nested on artificial rafts on occasions. Sand martins rear their broods in sandy river banks above Street Bridge, while other familiar species such as swift, swallow and house martin nest in structures created by man and fly low over the meres and the river in their quest for insects. A good selection of wintering wildfowl may be seen and even a red-throated diver has been known to grace this habitat.

The fishery is situated on the Duchy of Lancaster's Wyreside estate and across the river the landscape is dominated by Wyresdale Hall. Corless mill once stood several storeys high on the river bank and exploited children from Liverpool to weave wool and work the machines as cheap labour. Dolphinholme was originally Tolfinsholme, a Norse settlement. It seems that the name has its origins in a Norseman called Tolfin who happened to settle on a holme or river island. Dolphinholme's industrial origins are still evident and the factory used to employ 1400 people. With the coming of the Industrial Revolution, Dolphinholme (along with Preston) is said to have been one of the earliest places to be lit with gas during the first decades of the 19th Century.

Like Corless mill, several properties have today been converted to housing, yet the presence of screaming swifts flying over the village on a summer evening have preserved the essence of rural tranquillity. Long may they continue to do so!

Winter spectacular at Pilling

Wader flock

Start:	Start and return to Fluke Hall car park
Grid reference:	SD389500
Distance:	3 km (1.9 miles) – the extra suggestions are about 12 km (7.5 miles) by car
Grade:	Easy
General:	Toilets and other services in Pilling

♿ Wheelchair access to the sea wall at Fluke Hall and Lane Ends Amenity Area

THIS WALK GIVES EXCELLENT BIRD WATCHING from late July through to late May. However, the tidal section of the walk is very tide-dependent, featuring an unforgettable spectacle of tens of thousands of mixed waders gathering to roost as the tide displaces them from the inter-tidal area. When the tide is out they feed on the abundant invertebrates which occur in superabundance, which means that the waders congregate at high tide on any exposed sand bank, salt marsh or beach. So it is imperative to get the timing right and visit at the recommended times and state of the tide. Tidal timing and heights are available in most local papers, tide tables can be purchased from fishing shops, or alternatively tidal information can be found at www.pol.ac.uk/appl/liverpool.html.

The predictions and heights most readily available are those for Liverpool and they are very similar to those on the Lune estuary and are used in this walk. The tidal heights suitable to get the best bird watching are those above 8.5 metres. These occur around the middle of the day. Tidal height can be affected by weather conditions, with a strong westerly wind making the tide higher or calm anti-cyclonic conditions having the opposite effect.

1. *Park in the small car park at Fluke Hall, preferably two hours before high tide, and walk on top of the sea wall to the left, towards Knott End. DO NOT GO ONTO THE INTER-TIDAL AREA. Details of how far to walk are given below, depending on tide height and birds present.*

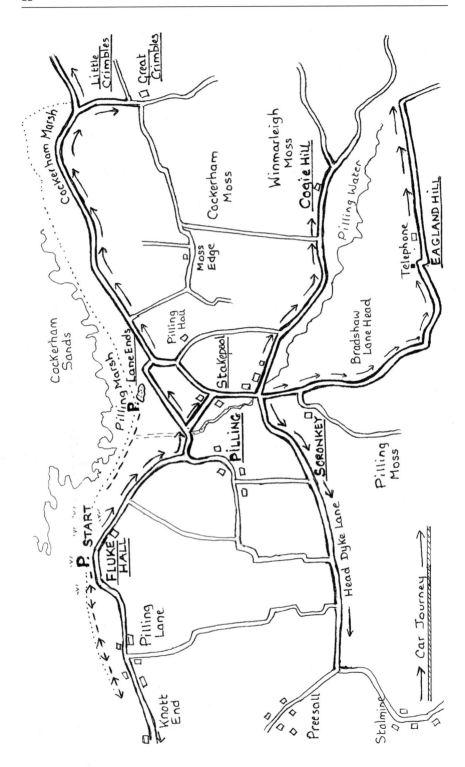

The fields behind the sea wall hold migrants in spring and autumn such as wheatear, meadow pipits, skylarks, linnets and twite. Large flocks of lapwing and, at times, golden plover and curlew, occur on these fields and some will have originated in Bowland. In winter huge flocks of pink-footed geese occur at times. They announce their presence usually before you spot them, especially if they have been disturbed. On the seaward side of the sea wall, depending on the wetness of the sand, small flocks of redshank and dunlin may be feeding. In some winters a small flock of snow buntings winters along the embankment. Check with binoculars regularly towards Knott End to watch for the wader flocks starting to assemble, which will show as a massed flock against the quickly moving tide-line. Walk down until you are opposite the first substantial flock. The distance you have to walk will depend on eventual tide height, weather conditions and, of course, the time you set out and how much there is to see on the way out. Once you have reached the flocks, the best plan is to slowly walk back, keeping up with the waders, which are being slowly forced towards you by the incoming tide.

Enjoy the spectacle of the massed throngs, especially thrilling when they take to flight, twisting and turning like animated smoke. Observe how the long-legged bar-tailed godwit and curlew stand further out in the water and next is a great pack of oystercatchers, with smaller numbers of grey plover and redshank with shorter legs. But closest of all are the vast throngs of knot dunlin and smaller numbers of ringed plover and sanderling, all with shorter legs and often still feeding. Numbers naturally vary depending on the season. August to early September can be very good for variety, especially as many adult birds are still in their bright breeding plumage. Remarkably, many of these waders have travelled from as far away as Arctic Canada, Greenland and Siberia. In many species the first birds to arrive back are the females, for they leave the male in charge of the young. However, the sanderling is unique for the female lays two clutches, one which she incubates and the other for the male to tend! Birds are not always able to breed success- fully each year in the high Arctic so the sanderling makes

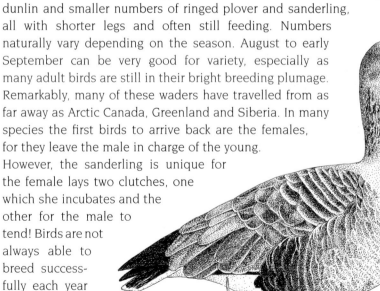

Pink footed goose

good use of those years when conditions are suitable. In late summer flocks of terns, mainly common, Arctic and sandwich, roost with the waders. All our regular land-based gull species also occur at this time.

The largest numbers of waders occur from mid-October onward, mainly because many knot, which moult along the North Sea coast, move to the west coast after completing their moult. Many species start to move out in late February, with oystercatchers being the first to leave. April and May produces passage ringed plover, dunlin and sanderling, many in full summer plumage. The latter has been shown to make the journey non-stop from Britain to Greenland, while some other species use Iceland as a re-fuelling halt. Indeed many of the birds at this time of year have wintered further south in Southern Europe or West Africa and they are using the inter-tidal areas of the Lune estuary as a stopping off point to refuel on the superabundant bi-valves and sand hoppers.

Where the waders roost at high tide will depend on the eventual height of the tide and also the level of disturbance, both human and avian. On tides below 9 metres they usually roost on the exposed sand to the south of Fluke Hall car park. On higher tides they flight to the large salt marsh upstream of the car park, best viewed by telescope from the sea wall at Fluke Hall. With the turn of the tide the waders become more settled and rest over the high tide until the sands are exposed again and they can resume feeding. However, the most breath-taking spectacle occurs when a peregrine or merlin 'beats up' the wader flock, causing them to twist and turn in superb unison. Despite the tens of thousands of potential prey, it is amazing how often the predators miss! But if and when they catch, they regularly fly to the salt marsh or sea wall to pluck unfortunate victims and peace returns to the flock, although if the attacks are sustained for any period, many waders, especially the smaller ones, will flight away across the estuary to find refuge. Returning to the car park, it is well worth looking over the hedge into the usually arable field. In winter this usually supports a mixed flock of greenfinch, chaffinch, linnet, twite and tree sparrow, and both grey and red-legged partridge are regular.

2. *Another excellent view of the wader roost is available from the east side by driving to Lane End's Amenity Area (see map), which has an excellent car park on top of the sea wall. It is quite possible to walk to this new site along the road, and past the Golden Ball Hotel; however, as time is of the essence before the high tide roost breaks up and winter days are short, driving is recommended.*

At times the major part of the wader roost is visible from this site. Walking back along the sea wall towards Fluke Hall produces a much closer view; however, rather strangely this part of the embankment is closed to public access from December 27th to Good Friday. Both grey and golden plover regularly roost on the salt marsh just out from the car park. It is also the best place to see wildfowl, which mainly congregate in the mouth of Pilling Water. Wigeon, mallard and shelduck are the commonest, but teal, shoveler, pintail and red-breasted merganser are usually present, with a small flock of wintering, dark-bellied brent geese. Flocks of pinkfeet regularly graze on the salt marsh or flight inland to the mossland fields round Pilling, or even to Marton Mere and the Ribble marshes. The tide-line attracts small flocks of skylarks and meadow pipits and at times brown hares can be seen retreating from the tide. Regularly visible raptors are peregrine, merlin, sparrowhawk and kestrel and less frequently hen harrier and short-eared owl.

3. *During winter and early spring the fields around Pilling are the feeding grounds of up to 10,000 pinkfeet, with the greatest numbers from early January to early March. The flocks are quite mobile and it is something of a wild goose chase to locate them. Again, driving is best, not only because a larger area can be covered but also at times the car makes a good hide. The best locations include Crimbles Lane, Scronkey, Cogie Hill and Eagland Hill. For details of how to reach these sites consult the map.*

Very often the first clue as to which area the pinkfeet are using is when they take to flight. With them, especially after the turn of the year, are small numbers of European white-fronted geese, whooper and Bewick's Swan, barnacle geese, as well as greylag and Canada. The area around Eagland Hill is favoured and in recent years this has proved even more attractive with the provision of feeding stations for wintering passerines. This excellent project, organised by Bob Danson, attracts large numbers of tree sparrows, yellow-hammers, corn buntings, and at times brambling, along with many of the common finches, to the two sites just off the road either side of Eagland Hill (see map). Other birds to watch for in winter include flocks of redwing and fieldfare, both partridges, merlin, sparrowhawk and little owl. If you linger on the mosses towards dusk there is a strong chance that an excellent day's bird watching will end on a high note with good views of a hunting barn owl.

Conder Green to Cockersands and return

Teal

Start: Start and return to Conder Green picnic site
Grid reference: SD457562
Distance: 12 km (7.5 miles)
Grade: Easy
General: Toilets in the picnic site – other services at
Conder Green and Glasson
♿ Wheelchair access to view the river at Conder
Green and Cockersands Lighthouse car park

AN OPPORTUNITY TO EXPLORE A LITTLE MORE of the Lune estuary which can be productive at all states of the tide, before returning via low-lying farmland. Beware though of extreme high spring tides (10 metres or more) which flood the road and can maroon you in the car park for an hour and always consult the tide tables before setting out.

1. *Follow the coastal footpath south out of the picnic site until a left turn across the round-about and over the canal bridge. Take the first right round the back of Glasson Marina and, at the next right-angle turn, take the footpath towards Crook Farm, then along the embankment ending opposite the lighthouse on Plover Scar near Cockersands. This section gives good views over the Lune estuary to Sunderland Point. Heysham nuclear power station rather dominates the distant view.*

Outside the breeding season this is an excellent area for flocks of lapwing and golden plover, on both the fields and the salt marsh. With them, especially in wet periods, will be smaller numbers of redshank, curlew, oystercatcher and occasionally dunlin and knot. The salt marsh supports good numbers of wigeon and shelduck. The embankment is an excellent vantage point for viewing the estuary. At low water and as the tide ebbs and flows, the sands and scars are sprinkled with small groups and flocks of dunlin, knot, oyster-catcher, curlew and redshank. The Cockersands area is also usually excellent for grey plover, bar-tailed and at times black-tailed godwits, turnstone, ringed plover and during spring and autumn passage, sanderling. On the

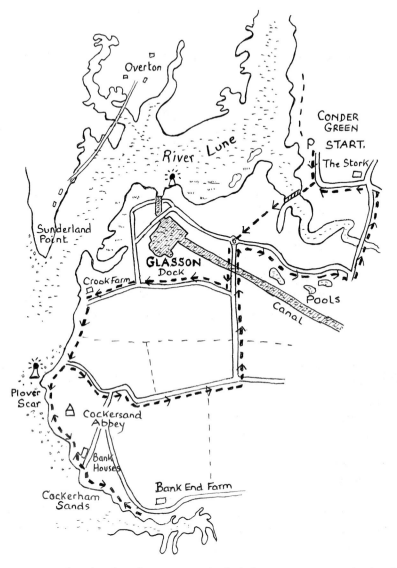

lower or neap tides the shingle spit near the lighthouse serves as a high tide roost for many of these waders, but on the higher or spring tides it is covered and the waders flight across the estuary to the large salt marsh to the west of Sunderland Point. The river channel is good at any state of the tide for red-breasted mergansers and at times goosanders, along with goldeneye and great crested grebe. Long-tailed ducks and the rarer grebes have also been recorded. From April to September terns can often be seen. Common terns are the most regular but Arctic, sandwich and little terns occur at passage times. Gale force winds also regularly blow in seabirds such as gannet, kittiwake and guillemot.

The fields behind the sea wall, besides holding the waders already mentioned, are good for wintering passerines, which are rather dependent on the cropping regime. Stubble fields are best and when conditions are right, flocks of skylarks, mixed finches, buntings and sparrows including twite, linnet and tree sparrow, are well worth searching for.

2. *Return past the small car park to the land-based lighthouse, now converted to a house, and take the road inland. Continue along this road inland until a left turn down Jeremy Lane, which returns you across the canal bridge to the roundabout. Here there is the option of going back to the car park along the coastal path or you can follow the road alongside the Conder crossing over the bridge, turning left at the Stork pub and back to the car park.*

The fields hold good numbers of the waders already described. Golden plover and lapwing often feed right up to the road. With them in winter are flocks of redwing and fieldfare and, as in the last section, if there is a stubble field this can be very good for winter passerines. Many of the fields are bordered by reed-filled ditches, in which breed reed buntings and sedge warblers. Merlins, peregrines and sparrowhawks often hunt these fields, while in late winter, flocks of pinkfeet visit. The fields either side of Jeremy Lane have in recent winters become good for wintering swans, with up to 70 mute swan and with them smaller numbers of Bewick's and whooper swans, which look rather out of place grazing on the lush grass, well away from water.

N.B.

Whooper swan

Abbeystead lake

grey wagtail

Start: Start at and return to the informal car park
near Stoops Bridge, Abbeystead

Grid reference: SD564544

Distance: 3 km (1.9 miles)

Time: Allow 2 to 3 hours

Grade: Easy

General: Public toilets and refreshment facilities at
Dunsop Bridge

THIS ATTRACTIVE WALK CIRCUMNAVIGATES the reservoir, passing through mature and wet woodland, open fields and the picturesque village of Abbeystead. Although the circular walk is rather short, it may be extended by going up or down stream on the River Wyre. It is possible to extend the walk by following the Wyre Way footpath downstream from below the dam and spillway to link up with walk No. 5 at Dolphinholme.

The path passes through mature, mainly oak woodland with alder along the river. In spring the woods are a riot of colour with bluebells and ransoms under the trees and marsh marigolds along the wet margins. Both grey wagtail and dipper can be found in the first section of the river. The mature woodland is ideal for redstart and pied flycatcher and a good variety of woodland birds, including chiffchaff, treecreeper, great spotted and green woodpeckers, marsh and long-tailed tits and nuthatch. Redpolls breed in the alder and willow scrub and are joined by siskin in winter. Buzzards often pass overhead giving their mewing call, while the harsh call of the raven announces its presence. The woodland path offers brief but rather tantalising views of the wetland through gaps in the trees; however there are better views ahead.

1. *The area around the dam and spillway usually provides excellent bird watching. By taking a very short and well-used diversion to the right of the main track at the start of the dam wall, it is possible to get excellent views over the lake. By standing or sitting quietly at this viewing point it is possible to see the lake, the fringing vegetation of aquatic plants and scrub and an excellent view over the spillway and down the river.*

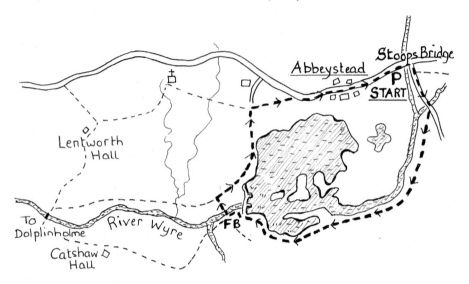

With expanses of both deep and shallow water, the lake attracts an impressive variety of birds, the most obvious being mute swan, grey lag and Canada geese, all of which breed around the lake. One or two pairs of great crested grebe are regular breeders. Always a joy to watch, this attractive species is easy to identify, with the erectile ear tufts and frill of summer plumage making it so distinctive. In spring they have elaborate courtship rituals including much bill fencing and mutual head shaking, often accompanied by raucous calling. The most elaborate display is known as the weed or penguin dance – both birds dive and bring up weed, approach each other and rise onto the water so that their breasts touch, maintaining this position for a few seconds before sinking back into the water. This truly spectacular courtship display can be difficult to see but is unforgettable. Little grebe also breed, though they can be quite secretive, and often the first clue to their presence is the rippling trill call.

Other breeding waterfowl include several pairs of mallard, tufted duck, coot and moorhen. Red-breasted merganser, teal and shelduck have bred in some years and are usually present in spring. Common sandpiper and oystercatcher breed on the exposed shoreline, while sedge warblers and reed bunting can be found in the extensive areas of aquatic vegetation and willow scrub. At times numbers of the three regular gull species, black-headed, lesser black-backed and herring, visit the lake to drink or bathe. Herons are regular fishers in the shallows. Under certain weather conditions, usually when colder weather means insects are hard to find elsewhere, large numbers of swifts, swallows, sand and house martins and swifts hawk emerging insects over the water.

In winter, certain wildfowl are regular, including teal, pochard, tufted duck, goldeneye and goosander, while snipe may be seen along muddy margins. Migrant waders such as greenshank, whimbrel, green sandpiper and ruff have been recorded in spring and late summer.

The spillway and river provide ideal conditions for both grey wagtail and dipper, the former regularly offering excellent views on the stone work and banks above the dam, whilst the dipper normally prefers the faster flowing water. With views from above, this is an excellent place to watch the feeding habits of this attractive and unique species, which both walks and dives into the water, quickly submerging and using its wings to swim underwater after its aquatic prey. Kingfishers occur at times but have not been proved to breed in recent years. Do not forget to scan the trees for woodland birds, as many of the ones seen in the first section occur here also, along with spotted flycatcher. This is also an excellent place to watch for dragon and damsel flies.

2. *Crossing the river by the footbridge, follow the tarmac road then the sign posted footpath through the fields, keeping as close as possible to the trees fringeing the lake. The foot path eventually joins the road where a right turn takes you through the hamlet of Abbeystead, returning to the parking place.*

This section produces mainly woodland birds. The mature trees and scrub around the lake and along the road support good numbers at any time of the year, including chiffchaff, blackcap, garden warbler and both of the common woodpeckers. Look out in the gardens and buildings in Abbeystead for swallows, house martins and spotted flycatchers. In winter, well-stocked garden feeders attract a host of tits and finches.

Walk 9 increases the chances of seeing many of the birds of Abbeystead, including waders and upland species and typical river birds especially dipper, grey wagtail and common sandpiper.

Green sandpiper

Abbeystead and the two River Wyres

Green hairstreak

Start: Start at and return to the informal car park
near Stoops Bridge, Abbeystead

Grid reference: SD564544

Distance: 10.5 km (6.5 miles)

Time: Allow 5 hours

Grade: Easy to moderate

General: Public toilets and refreshment facilities are at
Dunsop Bridge

THIS IS ANOTHER GREAT SCENIC CIRCULAR WALK, embracing diverse countryside with the backdrop of the Bowland fells. It provides an opportunity to spot several of Bowland's characteristic birds and the period late April or early May is recommended as the best time to do the walk. It follows the attractive riverine habitats of the two River Wyres, a traditional haunt of dipper, common sandpiper and grey wagtail. Tracing the actual source of the Wyre is not for the faint hearted because the two tributaries that form the main river originate high on the fells of Tarnbrook and Marshaw Fell respectively before reaching the confluence at Abbeystead. We will not be going to these sources, so conserve your energy and just enjoy the bird watching in a spectacular, historic landscape.

1. *The walk describes a circular extension of the Wyre Way walking outward to the Tarnbrook Wyre returning via the Marshaw Wyre. Follow the Wyre Way logo and Ordnance Survey Outdoor Leisure map 41. Walk east from Stoops Bridge leaving the main road at a bungalow (right) at the top of the hill. Follow the Wyre Way logo and yellow way markers across fields, keeping right of Higher Emmett's Farm and crossing the main road to arrive at 'Top of Emmetts.' Keep right of the building, following the line of the hedge to reach a cluster of three stiles. Veer left across a field heading towards a prominent barn and passing right alongside it. Follow a hedge (right) crossing several stiles and the Tarnbrook Wyre to arrive at the hamlet of Tarnbrook.*

Many species occur in the woodlands and open country along the route from Abbeystead and the remote hamlet of Tarnbrook, including song and mistle thrush, finches, titmice, robin, wren, reed bunting, pied and grey wagtail, jackdaw and the inevitable pheasant. Resident ravens are often seen or heard croaking high above, having extended their range into Bowland from the Lake District. Look out for stock doves which frequent several of the farm buildings, and in summer, swallows and swift.

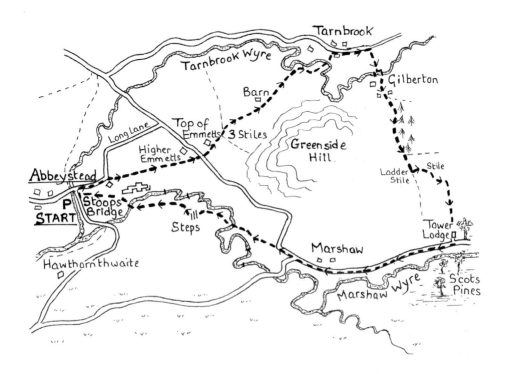

One is immediately struck by the breeding waders in many of the rough fields and in-bye. From early March to July curlew, lapwing, redshank and oystercatcher enhance the Bowland landscape with their vocal tones and presence. One of the first signs of spring is the bubbling quality of the curlew's repertoire that is both evocative and haunting, as it returns from the coast to traditional upland breeding grounds. Indeed the breeding lapwing and curlew population is one of the most significant in England. During the season both species may be seen performing their aerial displays while courageously mobbing any intruders such as crows and buzzards. Between October and April mixed flocks of fieldfares and redwings are commonly seen, often in large numbers before Christmas, and these roving flocks are likely to turn up almost anywhere, including flying over the fells. During

Scots Pines
Marshaw Wyre

C.Dodding

October skeins of pink-footed geese arrive from Icelandic breeding grounds, to wintering grounds at Over Wyre and may occasionally be seen flying in V formation over Bowland, usually as a result of disturbance on the feeding grounds. However, there is evidence that they follow a flight line over parts of the Forest of Bowland while en route to, or from, the east coast and traditional haunts in East Anglia. Pinkfeet also regularly commute between the fields of Cockerham and Winmarleigh Moss and the traditional safe haven at Martin Mere and the mosslands of south west Lancashire and Merseyside.

2. *At Tarnbrook turn right along the track and where it divides, take the right fork, turning left over a footbridge preceding farm buildings. On reaching two barns take the right hand gate and head up Speight's Clough, passing a plantation (left) and stile/gate, proceeding onto open moorland near Greenside. At this point use binoculars to reveal well hidden yellow way-markers and the location of equally obscure wall stiles. Cross over the moor heading towards a substantial track bearing a finger post above Tower Lodge.*

3. *Turn right on the track to Tower Lodge and right again along the main road for approximately two miles. Carry straight on past a road junction (left) and shortly thereafter regain the Wyre Way footpath. Follow the yellow way markers back to Stoops Bridge,* *crossing over several footbridges straddling the Marshaw Wyre. After climbing up some stone steps, gain a good view of Abbeystead Mansion, the country seat of the Duke of Westminster.*

After discovering the hamlet of Tarnbrook we again cross the Tarnbrook Wyre where the route ascends higher ground. Here flocks of introduced red-legged partridge abound and perky spring wheatears feed in the fields and nest in the walls. Both redstart and pied wagtail also use holes for nesting, whilst away from the silage fields, meadow pipit play host to the cuckoo which, although far less numerous than formerly, may still be seen and heard as a harbinger of spring. Despite the redstart's superb colouration it can be elusive, but in spring the singing male may be located by the rather feeble whirring song delivered from high up in dense foliage in upland plantations such as that at 'Harry Wood'. Scattered trees and woodland margins are also the preferred haunt of the tree pipit, another declining species that may still be seen in favoured localities performing its vocal aerial display and parachuting down from a tree or wire in spring-time. Watch out for stonechat that has expanded its range into the upland areas of Bowland and is now more frequently observed in heather and tall bracken than its close relative the whinchat. The cuckoo and ring ousel seem to be rapidly gaining the dubious status of 'uncommon' in many former haunts, although on this walk it may be possible to hear a cuckoo or observe a ring ousel moving to higher ground in early spring.

One possible cause of the reduction in summer migrants to Britain, such as the cuckoo, tree pipit, whinchat and ring ousel, could be that something tragic is happening on the wintering grounds or during migration; for example changes in agricultural practice in Third World countries or the indiscriminate shooting and trapping of millions of birds in Mediterranean countries such as Malta.

Redshank

Close to Tower Lodge in the Trough of Bowland we gain the Marshaw Wyre, where there is a wonderful stand of Scots pine, which occasionally attracts flocks of crossbill and other coniferous loving species such as goldcrest, coal tit, siskin and lesser redpoll. During 'crossbill invasions' the cone-bearing trees support noisy flocks – winter and early spring are the best times to look for the distinctive red males and green females with their intriguing cross bills of the lower and upper mandible. The Trough road at Marshaw is a good vantage point to watch for red grouse that are commonly seen in the heather areas but never in the lowlands.

Sightings of red kite are increasing throughout the Bowland area as a result of successful introduction schemes elsewhere in Britain. Scanning the heather moorland areas for raptors usually produces the best results in spring and may reveal a handsome male hen harrier, quartering the heather or indulging in a display known as 'skydancing', while making a food-pass to the contrasting brown coloured female. The much smaller merlin uses its superb turn of speed to fly down its main prey, the meadow pipit. Peregrines are now quite well established in the Forest of Bowland and in late spring families can be seen together in the sky, giving superb, vocal aerial displays. Hunting peregrines are masters of the sky, renowned for attacking prey from above at speeds of around 200mph. This is also prime habitat for the diurnal hunting short-eared owl, whose population fluctuates, the greatest numbers occurring in years when voles are abundant. The distinctive shape and rounded wings of a sparrowhawk may be glimpsed flying across the open fell, before disappearing into a plantation while hunting small birds. By contrast, the kestrel or windhover provides more opportunity for observation as it hovers over the fell with eyes focussed on small mammalian prey. Buzzards with their plaintive mewing call are now well established throughout the area, with rabbits featuring prominently on their menu.

Descending along the wooded valley of the Marshaw Wyre, look and listen for pied and spotted flycatchers, redstart and warblers. Warblers tend to skulk but their distinctive songs help to locate them. As you walk, blackcap, garden warbler, chiffchaff and willow warbler sing from the trees and thickets. Their distinctive songs are worth taking the trouble to learn as a means of identification. This account has mainly alluded to birding in Bowland during early spring but in winter you can equally enjoy a 'nice walk,' especially when the weather is crisp and bright. Although the bird scene may be rather quiet there will always be something to watch, if only the superb changing landscapes!

Red-legged partridge

A single ticket from Lancaster to Conder Green

N.B.   Kingfisher

Start:	Start at St George's Quay, Lancaster, finish Conder Green
Grid reference:	SD 474623
Distance:	9 km (5.9 miles)
Time:	4 to 5 hours
Grade:	Easy
General:	Toilet and refreshment facilities available at Lancaster and Conder Green
	Wheelchair access and facilities are provided from Conder Green to Aldcliffe

THIS WALK ALONG THE LANCASHIRE COASTAL WAY parallels the course of the River Lune, beginning at the historic St George's Quay, Lancaster, and ending at Conder Green. A longer return walk featuring the Lancaster canal towpath to Galgate may be considered. At both Conder Green and Galgate buses serve Lancaster for the return journey. Alternatively, a shorter evening or daytime walk may be taken from the Conder Green car park – just go as far as you want in either direction within your available time.

Before commencing the walk at St George's Quay, it is worth reflecting on the local history associated with the walk. Today Carlisle Bridge carries the main Anglo-Scottish railway line but close by in medieval times was the site of a wooden structure known as Loyne Bridge. Maintenance problems in 1252 were such that King John ordered that twenty oaks should be cut down to repair it. St George's Quay houses the Lancaster Maritime Museum in the Old Custom House and during the 17th century Lancaster traded with

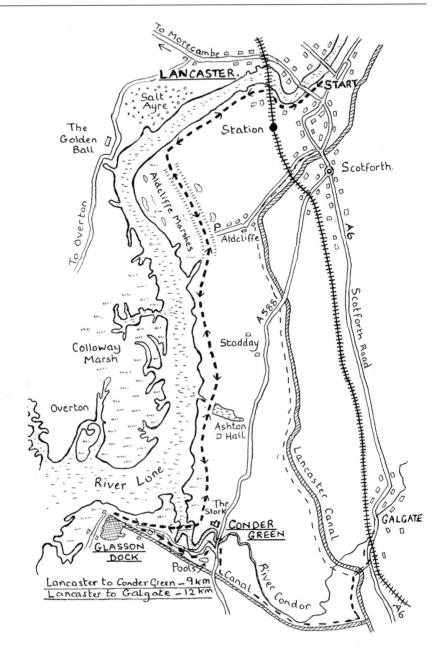

the Baltic and West Indies from ports at the Quay and Sunderland Point. The first recorded voyage from Lancaster was to Jamaica in the West Indies undertaken by a 50 ton cargo vessel, 'The Lamb', in 1687. It was not until 1787 that Glasson Dock was built and today this busy little port is a hive of activity for both pleasure craft and commercial shipping.

For this walk we have a single ticket to Conder Green, with an option to extend to Glasson Dock, to view the birds along the route of the former Glasson Dock Railway. Conder Green was the only intermediate station on the line and beyond Glasson Dock station were the sidings that served the basins and quays. Like so many other defunct railway lines it is now in effect a linear nature reserve and it is integrated into the River Lune Millennium Park. The old railway has been reinvented as a right of way and cycleway, affording good views of the River Lune but what of its nostalgic past?

Between 1845 and 1848 various proposals for linking the dock with the Lancaster and Preston Junction Railway and the Lancaster quays were made. These proposals were successfully opposed by the powerful Lancaster Canal Company, which had constructed a canal branch to the dock in 1826 and must have thought they could compete with the impact of the iron horse instead of the trusty steed on the towpath – some hope! However, no real progress on the railway proposal was made until 1871 and it was not until July, 1883, that the branch was opened by the L.N.W.R. In 1883 there were four trains daily on the branch and when passenger services were withdrawn, as an early casualty of closures, on the 7th July 1930, there were still four trains daily in each direction with an additional three trains on Saturdays. Trains took fifteen minutes for the five mile journey. With the last freight train trundling along the branch at its maximum permitted speed of 30 miles per hour, in 1964 the Glasson Dock Branch line was consigned to the annals of nostalgic railway history. Fortunately, the elevated Victorian anachronism of a track-bed lives on and affords good birding with a diversity of habitats. The Lune estuary is designated as a Special Protection Area and Site of Special Scientific Interest and comprises grazed and un-grazed salt marsh, sandflats and tidal creeks. The Conder estuary is the only muddy area on the east of Morecambe Bay and holds a good variety of waders at most states of the tide, especially low water.

The tidal heights suitable to get the best bird watching are mid-day tides of around 9 metres. The most productive time to commence the walk is approximately two hours before high tide with the aim of being at Aldcliffe Marsh for high tide and at Conder Green as the tide ebbs, thus exposing intertidal mud flats.

1. *From the quay follow the coastal way footpath logo south past the Lancaster Industrial Estate towards Conder Green/Glasson Dock and unfortunately along a road used by heavy lorries. After the grime of suburbia the road eventually narrows into a footpath indicated by a sign 'Glasson, Conder Green Aldcliffe'. Follow the track for approximately ½ kilometre to a junction with a sign indicating Marsh Point. Take this right tree-lined elevated path to reach Aldcliffe Marsh. Turn left and proceed south along the bank to a small car park situated adjacent to the old railway track-bed at Level Crossing Lane.*

Follow the well signed route along the old track, watching out for the ghost train! Walk the line south to Conder Green, eventually passing through a cutting with an over-bridge.

Nowadays, in geomorphologic terms the River Lune is a fine river where redshank, oystercatcher, lapwing, goosander, goldeneye, mallard and gulls are frequently observed from Lancaster's well known bridges, as well as St George's Quay. At Aldcliffe Marsh, there is a chance of finding something good, particularly if your timing coincides with high tide. From here on the elevated coastal path is situated betwixt hedgerow and a substantial tide-line. The fields and tide-line hold migrants in spring and autumn such as wheatear and meadow pipits, while on the landward side extensive fields with ditches and pools harbour reed buntings, moorhen and skylark and wintering snipe and green sandpiper. Other winter visitors are sometimes represented in the hedge and or tide-line by flocks of brambling and chaffinch, flocks of redwing and fieldfare, linnet and twite and singular rock pipits that usually signal their presence with a distinctive 'peest' call – or words to that effect depending on perceptions!

The path affords good views of Aldcliffe salt marsh which supports large numbers of curlew, oystercatcher, lapwing, golden plover, grey plover, redshank, dunlin and wildfowl, along with flocks of mallard, shelduck, wigeon, pintail and teal. In addition to the regular mute swan flock there are smaller numbers of wintering whooper and bewick swans and thus there is a chance of observing all three species of swan at the same time. Large flocks of pink-footed geese are present from January to March and are sometimes joined by smaller numbers of bean, white-fronted and brent geese, along with larger numbers of feral grey lag and Canada geese.

A measure of skill is required to distinguish the visiting raptors that pursue the waders and wildfowl. The marsh is frequented by the familiar kestrel, characteristically hovering in search of small mammals. Aerial pursuits of waders and wildfowl caused by visiting raptors are quite dramatic to watch as they disturb the serenity of the marshes. Look skywards or scan the marsh for signs of disturbance to the wader flocks, a sure sign that either merlin or peregrine may be on patrol, producing utter mayhem and thus contributing greatly to the day's overall enjoyment! A less dramatic wader reaction is caused by occasional hunting hen harrier, short-eared owl and the commoner sparrowhawk.

The old railway track banks and path edges are excellent for butterflies, including small copper, wall brown, grayling and common blue in season. The distance between Aldcliffe car park and Ashton Hall is about two kilometres and during spring time the extensive bushes and trees come alive with the songs of willow warbler, blackcap, whitethroat and lesser whitethroat. In winter there are invariably innumerable lapwing, golden plover and wigeon on the sand adjacent to the main river channel and on the marshes. Whatever the season it is a good time to take advantage of the numerous strategically placed wooden benches to see what you can find while perhaps partaking of lunch.

At Stodday note the remains of a private platform used in earlier years by the late Lord Ashton when in residence at Ashton Hall. This palatial former residence with its own heronry is now the headquarters of the Lancaster Golf Club. Close by a tributary of the Lune drains an ornamental lake and passes under the railway. Streams such as this are often used by grey wagtail and kingfisher as favourable coastal habitat during winter, so look out for and respond to that quick flash of blue! Little egrets are on the increase, possibly as a result of global warming and, at the time of writing, up to ten birds can be seen flying to their inland roost close to the river. Further south is a small peninsula where a high tide roost of oystercatcher, redshank, knot, ringed plover, dunlin, curlew and bar-tailed godwit may be observed. Cormorants regularly fish the channel and stand around motionless in their characteristic pose.

2. *On reaching the site of Conder Green station just south of the car park/public toilets and amenity area, the River Conder is crossed on an iron girder viaduct. After the viaduct the railway track commences a sharp curve on an embankment that led to the site of Glasson Dock station. Go left on the main road and continue over the road bridge, turning left past the Stork Pub and back towards the car park to see another section of the exposed mud, 'up the creek'. Retrace your steps to the Stork Inn to catch a bus back to Lancaster or commence walking to Galgate along the canal towpath.*

The bushes and hedges bordering the railway and amenity area around Conder Green should not be neglected. House and tree sparrows are regular, while in late summer, migrant warblers may be spotted in the bushes. In winter the salt marshes hold variable numbers of reed bunting, twite and linnet.

From the slightly elevated area by the picnic tables there is a good view across the salt marsh to the Lune estuary where a telescope is advisable to aid identification. From here, merlins may sometimes be seen utilising the masts of beached boats as a look-out. The exposed salt flats and mussel beds attract flocks of dunlin, redshank, bar-tailed godwit, turnstone, and ringed plover. Whimbrel are regular on the marshes in May and autumn, with greenshanks mainly occurring from July to September. At any state of the tide red-breasted mergansers, along with goldeneye, great crested grebe, and the rarer grebes, have also been recorded. From April to September terns can often be seen. Common terns are the most regular but Arctic, sandwich and little tern also occur. Along the river herons stalk in the shallows while goosanders fish in the deeper sections.

With a telescope it is possible to check the salt marsh on the north side of the Lune. In spring and early summer common terns often nest here. In late winter flocks of pinkfeet with a few whitefronts and wild swans, both whooper and Bewick's, occur, while wigeon graze the salt marsh. In early summer crèches of young shelduck assemble, supervised by a few adults, while the rest of the adult population make a moult migration to the Heligoland Bight in Germany, before returning in late September in pristine new dress.

The confluence of the Conder with the Lune and the immediate area of ungrazed salt marshes are rich in botanical interest with thrift, sea arrow grass, sea milkwort, sea purslane, common sea lavender and the rare lax flowered sea lavender. On the avian front, the marshes and the muddy Conder creek have an impressive list of rarities. The white-winged black tern, a rare vagrant from Eastern Europe, has topped the bill in recent years with a supporting cast of black terns and little gulls and interesting passage waders. Good views of the River Conder are afforded from the viaduct, embankment and road. The peak of the autumn passage usually extends from early August to October and common sandpiper, green sandpiper, wood sandpiper, ruff, greenshank, spotted redshank, both species of godwit and whimbrel are typically seen. In good years some little stint and curlew sandpiper occur, with a few adults in late July/early August and larger numbers of juveniles moving through in September. Birds that frequent the muddy creek at Conder Green include grey plover, turnstone, redshank, curlew, snipe, dunlin, teal, mallard, shelduck and heron. The creek is one of the easiest places in the area to see kingfisher, which are regular outside the breeding season with up to two or three birds regularly using the boats or posts as fishing perches. At every opportunity, discreetly scope the extreme course of the meandering creek from afar, trying not to upset that sentinel of the marsh, the redshank, whose strident vocalisations will quickly transform it into a somewhat birdless scenario, apart from perhaps a few starlings behaving like waders searching for rich pickings in the soft mud!

Check the newly excavated pool to the south of the road where there is a raised platform designed to aid watching. This site has thus far demonstrated its bird watching potential with many of the species already listed, plus rarer species such as little ringed plover, scaup, long-tailed duck and vagrants from the Americas such as pectoral sandpiper. On the walk back towards the Stork pub the stretch of river upstream from the road bridge is a favoured site for green sandpiper. As well as the usual suspects the Conder Estuary also attracts wintering spotted redshank and greenshank, which on a cold winter's day provide a bonus worthy of a celebratory tipple at the nearest hostelry.

The River Lune ramble: Arkholme to Kirkby Lonsdale

Goosander N.B.

Start: Starts at Arkholme and finishes at Kirkby Lonsdale
Grid reference: SD 589718
Distance: 8 km (5.3 miles)
Time: Allow 5 to 6 hours
Grade: Easy
General: Toilets and refreshments at Devil's Bridge and in Kirkby Lonsdale

THIS WALK TAKES IN CONTRASTING parts of the river, from the wide, slow flowing section with its shingle beds and sandy banks near Arkholme, to the faster flowing, upper reaches further upstream near Kirkby Lonsdale. It should produce a very good selection of typical river birds. The walk starts at Arkholme and finishes at Kirkby Lonsdale. Bus services are available between both sites so it would be possible to time your walk to fit in with these or make other arrangements to return.

1. *From the bus stop in the village centre, walk down the main street towards the river. Limited roadside parking is available at the river end of Arkholme's main street. Follow the path alongside the church and towards and under the railway viaduct.*

After leaving the village with its well stocked bird feeders, attracting several common species and siskin and brambling, the first section of the walk is alongside woodland and scrub with fields on the other side. Breeding birds include garden warbler, blackcap, treecreeper, great spotted woodpecker, nuthatch and long-tailed tit. Throughout the year birds are always plentiful, no doubt attracted by the river and its host of insects. In winter the fields

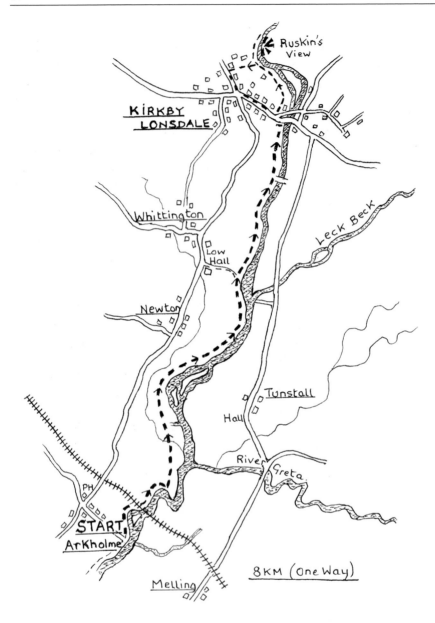

are well used by flocks of fieldfare and redwing, especially later in the winter when the berry crop has been exhausted.

The first good view of the river is just as you approach the viaduct, where a strategically placed seat allows excellent views downstream. Perseverance usually produces a kingfisher, often just a flash of blue as it speeds over the river. Kingfishers perch on both overhanging branches and stones so it is best to scan suitable sites and especially in the breeding season they can be very active. Scanning the calmer deeper water, a little distance down, usually reveals the first goosanders, easy to pick out on size alone from the mallard, little grebe, moorhen and coot which are also regular. Grey wagtails favour the fast flowing water near the viaduct and dippers used to be regular but seem to have disappeared as breeders in recent years, especially since the viaduct was re-pointed and generally tidied up.

Looking upstream from under the viaduct gives the first view of the shingle beds which are so much a feature of this section of the Lune. The river is constantly changing its course so the beds and sandy banks can change from year to year. Birds of this area include oystercatcher, teal, redshank, heron and common sandpiper.

2. *From the viaduct follow the track along the edge of the wood through the farmyard of Lower Broomfield Farm and on upstream. The path is well marked and the side streams are bridged. There are many advantageous viewing points of the river along this section, allowing views across stretches of shingle, sandy bank and low lying fields.*

The breeding bird of the shingle is the attractive black and white oyster-catcher, whose noisy 'piping' parties take place from late January to early July. This display is all part of the territorial disputes, and an integral part of the breeding behaviour of this wader. Many pairs nest on the bare shingle areas but in recent years almost all the shingle nesting population have had little success. Following heavy rain their nests are frequently washed out by the quickly rising flood water. The pairs nesting away from the river in the surrounding fields are usually more successful, as are pairs which have been encouraged to nest on special platforms provided for them on fence posts, therefore out of reach of most floods.

Other shingle nesting species include both ringed plover and little ringed plover, although numbers of the former have declined in recent years, again due to flooding. Where the shingle is higher and more vegetated and on into the adjacent fields, common sandpiper, lapwing, redshank and curlew all nest. A few pairs of the sadly declining yellow wagtail still breed in the same area. Of the wildfowl, mallard are the commonest followed by shelduck and goosander and a few pairs of tufted duck. Goosanders nest high up in large holes in trees or special nest boxes, though only the female incubates. On hatching, the youngsters simply jump out, hopefully onto a soft landing on water. As they grow several broods can be amalgamated to form a crèche but by this time only the females are left, the males having undertaken a moult migration. Surprisingly, ringing has shown that many travel as far as Norway just to renew their feathers!

The most abundant breeding bird along the river is the sand martin which excavates holes in the sandy banks. The position of colonies varies from year to year depending on the erosion of the bank, as they prefer a high vertical

Devil's Bridge.
Kirkby Lonsdale.   C. Dodding.

bank often with water below. At the time of writing there are two large colonies on the section upstream of Lower Broomfield Farm, one on each bank. Always a hive of activity, the best time to visit is probably the second half of April when the birds are busy excavating their arm-long holes. The Lune Valley is very much on a migration route and in spring and late summer osprey, marsh harrier and black tern, along with a seasonal passage of green sandpiper, greenshank, dunlin and spotted redshank, have all occurred.

In winter only a few of the breeding birds are left but these do include two of the most colourful – kingfisher and goosander. Winter wildfowl include large numbers of wigeon and teal along with flocks of Canada and greylag geese. The adjoining fields support large flocks of lapwing and at times golden plover and curlew. Most of these birds spread out to graze or feed on the pastures at the edge of the river but at times they gather to roost on the river shingle where they are often joined by flocks of black-headed and common gulls and smaller numbers of lesser black-backed and herring gulls. Green sandpipers have wintered along this stretch of the river. Several patches of alder occur close to the path and these are well worth searching for wintering redpolls and siskin, whilst other possible sightings include tree sparrow and little owl.

3. *Follow the path by the river under the pipe bridge. This aqueduct carries much of Manchester's water from the Lake District. Continue up to the new road bridge at Kirkby Lonsdale.*

Here the valley is narrower and there are fewer low lying fields. By now the shingle banks are much smaller and there are fewer trees. These changes in habitat mean that birds which favour the large shingle banks, such as ringed plover no longer occur but as the river flows faster grey wagtails become commoner. Oystercatcher, though, are still common, as are sand martins, although numbers have declined in recent years. In the late 1990s this section had the largest colony on the Lune with well over 400 holes, but work by the Environment Agency to stop erosion has altered the course of the river away from the bank reducing the colony to around 150 pairs. The shingle area that they created in doing this work was well used by nesting oystercatchers, being above flood level. However, in recent years they have declined due to the encroachment of Himalayan balsam or 'policeman's helmet' as it is popularly known. This showy alien has colonised many areas and is now the commonest flowering plant along the river. The first dipper is usually found on the section between the pipe bridge and the road bridge. Pied wagtails are one of the commonest breeding birds and there are usually two pairs of kingfisher and similar numbers of common sandpiper.

Winter wildfowl and water birds consist of large numbers of mallard and smaller numbers of goosander, goldeneye and a few little grebe and moorhen. Oystercatchers start to arrive in late January and this section of the Lune seems to serve as a gathering point at the start of the breeding season, with up to 250 regularly present in one favoured field on the south bank just above Leck Beck. The same field is also used in winter and at passage periods as a loafing or resting area for black-headed, common and a few lesser black-backed gulls.

4. *Take care in crossing the busy A65 and follow the path to Devil's Bridge. A short diversion onto the bridge is recommended before continuing along the riverside path and making your way up to Kirkby Lonsdale. There are two ways up the steep incline to the town. The first and easier ascent takes the rather narrow road just past the first house. The alternative route climbs a flight of steep steps and brings you to the famous Ruskin's view and the parish church.*

Yellow Wagtail

The mellowed and wonderfully attractive Devil's Bridge is a well known landmark. Myth has it that the bridge was built in a night by the Devil but he was cheated out of the soul of the first person to cross by a quick thinking townswoman. By contrast, an inscription high up on the bridge says, 'Fear God, honour the King 1633'.

This well wooded section is a very popular walk but most birds here are very tolerant of people. On the river look out especially for dippers, goosanders and grey wagtails throughout the year and common sandpipers in spring and summer. Woodland birds include nuthatch, great spotted woodpecker, many tits and, in spring and summer, blackcap, garden warbler and chiffchaff. In recent years there have been two or three pairs of the declining spotted flycatcher along the last section opposite the wooded island.

If you take the steps you can admire Ruskin's view and see if you agree with his sentiments, "I do not know in my own country, still less in France or Italy, a place more naturally divine."

Wigeon

The wigeon is the commonest of our wintering ducks occurring in large flocks around much of the coast with concentrations at South Walney and the Leven, Kent, Keer and Lune estuaries. Mid-winter counts suggest a population of about 6500 along the coast. It is also found in smaller numbers on inland waters and river valleys. This common winter visitor and passage migrant starts to arrive in August but the largest numbers arrive in late September and October. Numbers remain high throughout the winter but start to decline in late February with only small numbers left by mid-April. A very few either young or

S. Craig

injured birds remain through the summer. Ringing has shown that the bulk of our wintering birds breed across Northern Europe and into Russia with some coming from Iceland.

Its rather short pale blue bill is designed for grazing, especially on the short turf of the salt marshes. When not disturbed by shooting, at favoured haunts on nature reserves it will graze by day, but where it is persecuted it is mainly a night time feeder, particularly on moonlight nights. A flock of grazing wigeon is a wonderful sight enhanced by the evocative whistle of the males.

Walk numbers 1, 2, 3, 6, 7, 10, 11, 12, 13, 15, 16, 18, 22, 23, 24, 26, 27

Shoveler

D. Mower

The long, broad spatulate bill from which it takes its name is the most notable feature of this rather local and, in the case of the drake, colourful duck. The main population throughout the year is centred on the shallow lagoons at Leighton Moss and the adjacent brackish pools, with only small numbers being seen on other waters. It uses its large bill very effectively to sieve the water by drawing water rapidly through its bill and straining out the crustaceans and other fresh water invertebrates before expelling the water at the base of the bill. When feeding it is very active, often doing so in small groups which circle round each other. In nuptial display both birds rapidly bob their heads up and down in a rather comical manner. At times several drake will court a single duck with the same exaggerated head bobbing, after which the duck often takes to the wing to be pursued by her eager suitors.

Walk numbers 1, 2, 3, 4, 5, 8, 10, 13, 15, 16, 19, 23, 24, 26, 27

Dunlin

The dunlin is the commonest of the smaller waders and is present throughout the year, for even in late spring and summer small numbers of non-breeding birds remain. An average winter population is about 25,000. In winter plumage the dunlin has white under parts and grey upper parts, whilst in summer it is handsome in its rich reddish-brown upper parts and a black belly. It is also a most variable wader, however, both in colour, body size and, perhaps above all, bill length. The reason for this variability is that birds from several areas of its wide breeding range occur in the bay. Ringing returns have helped to work out which races occur, with birds from Siberia and northern Scandinavia making up the wintering population. Breeding birds from southern Scandinavia, Iceland and Greenland occur as passage migrants on their way to the wintering areas in Southern Europe and West Africa.

Like the knot this species engages in aerial manoeuvres when large flocks twist and turn, then drop like silvery rain. Because each bird turns at the same moment, a distant flock twisting against a light sky momentarily becomes invisible as the lighter under parts are turned towards the observer.

It is an active feeder spreading in flocks across the sand banks and wading in the shallow water continually probing for the abundant invertebrates. It never packs as closely as the knot and often feeds right up to high tide, while the knot stops feeding at least an hour before high tide.

Walk numbers 1, 2, 3, 6, 7,10, 12, 13, 16, 18, 22, 23, 24, 26, 27, 29

S. Craig

S. Craig

Ringed plover

The ringed plover is a breeding resident, a common passage migrant and a winter visitor in small numbers. Breeding is restricted to the shingle beaches and certain salt marshes as well as shingle banks adjacent to the River Lune. Nests are a simple scrape lined with a few small stones or broken shells. The anxious parents keep up a persistent, rather plaintive note if they are disturbed. When close to hatching or with young these courageous birds will use the broken wing routine to try to distract a potential predator.

The largest numbers of ringed plover pass through the bay during May when our local birds are already incubating eggs. Ringing has shown that these birds are bound for their breeding grounds in Iceland and Greenland. Return passage starts in August and continues until early October. This migrant population winters mainly in West Africa. They use the bay purely as a re-fuelling halt on their long journeys. Largest numbers are to be found along the Furness coast, at Walney and on the Lune estuary. The winter population is quite small, usually around 300–350 birds.

In a mixed flock of small waders ringed plover are easy to pick out by their feeding actions. They run a short distance, stop, observe, then pick up a small morsel such as a snail or sand hopper, and then run again. The short bill is designed for taking invertebrates near the surface.

Walk numbers 1, 2, 3, 6, 7, 12, 13, 10, 16, 18, 22, 23, 24, 26, 27, 29

D. Mower

Oystercatcher

The oystercatcher is one of most familiar and easily recognizable waders on Morecambe Bay. It is a common winter visitor with counts of around 50,000 in mid-winter, the largest concentration in Britain. Ringing has established that the breeding areas are in Iceland, the Faeroes, Norway and Scotland.

The resident population nests mainly on the shingle beaches and salt marshes but an expanding population is now well established inland on river shingle banks and farmland. The nest is just a scrape in the shingle or turf and lined with a few choice pebbles, shells or grasses. When breeding, they are very noisy, especially when they display in small 'piping parties', an extravagance of loud continuous calls which end in a quivering trill, delivered as the birds march round each other with the bill pointed downwards. These are probably neighbours arguing over territorial boundaries.

They feed largely on mussels and cockles and the large stout bill is ideal for retrieving and opening the usually abundant bi-valves. Feeding takes place at low water, both during the day and night. During wet spells, or when bi-valves are scarce, numbers move inland to feed on earthworms.

Walk numbers 1, 2, 3, 4, 5, 6, 7, 8, 9, 10, 11, 12, 13, 16, 18, 19, 22, 23, 24, 26, 27, 29

Black-tailed godwit (opposite)

The status of this elegant wader has changed markedly in recent years. Fifteen years ago it was only a spring and autumn passage migrant in small numbers with peak counts rarely exceeding ten. Now up to 700 winter on the specially created brackish pools and salt marsh areas centred on the Eric Morecambe lagoon. Smaller numbers can be found on the Lune estuary and at Hodbarrow RSPB Reserve. Ringing has shown that birds occurring in the bay breed in Iceland and many winter in France

In flight this large wader is easily identified from the bar-tailed godwit by its striking white wing bar. The sombre grey winter plumage contrasts with the superb chestnut breeding plumage which is donned during April and May. A few birds remain throughout the summer and the wintering population returns from early August.

Walk numbers 1, 2, 3, 7, 10, 12, 13, 15, 16, 18, 22, 23, 24, 26, 27

Redshank

S. Craig

The noisy, restless redshank breeds on many of the larger salt marshes and on marshy areas inland, although it has declined in these habitats in recent years due to land drainage. It is still however a reasonably common breeding bird in Bowland. It has a wonderful display flight where the male dances in the air on quivering wings, rising and falling above the female and keeping up a continual trilling call. The nest is well concealed in grasses or rushes.

The redshank is also a passage migrant and winter visitor with peak numbers during spring and autumn. The wintering population is usually around 7000 and large numbers are typically found at all high tide roosts, where they form rather discreet flocks often a little distance from the other waders. Ringing has shown that many of these birds breed in Iceland and Scandinavia. During wet spells, when many coastal fields are flooded, large numbers move to this new source of food. At low water many birds feed in the tidal creeks where their main prey is the sandhopper *Corophium* which lives in U-shaped burrows in the wet sand.

When alarmed the redshank adopts a bobbing motion and readily take to the wing, calling loudly and displaying the conspicuous white trailing edge to the wing, thus living up to its name as the 'sentinel of the marsh'

Walk numbers 1, 2, 3, 4, 5, 6, 7, 8, 9, 10, 11, 12, 13, 15, 16, 18, 19, 22, 23, 24, 26, 27, 29

C. Batty

sanderling

Sanderling

When feeding sanderling are one of the most active waders. They energetically chase sand hoppers, often at the edge of the tide, and are constantly on the move. The wintering population is sparse, with usually no more than 750 birds. The most favoured areas are the west side of Walney Island especially near the Biggar golf course and the Duddon and Wyre estuaries.

Spring passage starts in late April but peaks in late May and early June when up 15,000 have been recorded, the majority in the striking chestnut breeding plumage. Concentrations occur on the Lune and Duddon estuaries and along the west coast of Walney. Ringing has shown that many of these birds winter in Southern Europe and West Africa. In spring they are using the bay as a brief re-fuelling halt before setting out on the last leg of their journey, a non-stop flight to the breeding grounds which ringing returns have shown to be Greenland and across into Arctic Canada. Smaller numbers are recorded on the return passage; again ringing returns have revealed that many birds which use the west coast on the northern migration return via the North Sea coastline in the autumn.

Walk numbers 1, 2, 3, 6, 7, 10, 12, 13, 18, 22, 24, 26

Bearded tit

This wonderfully colourful resident is restricted to the extensive reed beds of Leighton Moss where the breeding population has varied between 65 and 7 pairs in recent years. The decline to just 7 pairs occurred during the 2000/2001 winter and has been attributed to a combination of prolonged high water levels followed by a cold snowy spell.

This can be rather a difficult species to find. Look out for them when the adults are feeding young from mid-April to late July and they can be seen carrying food across the top of the reeds. From June on the distinctively plumaged young start to flock and at times are quite obvious. But perhaps the easiest time is from late September to late November when the birds are collecting grit. Two grit trays have been put out just off the public footpath which runs right across the reserve, and small groups visit to stock up on grit, so a morning visit on a bright day is recommended. They need grit at this time of year as they are changing from the soft insect food of spring and summer to the much harder reed seed diet of winter.

Unlike many other passerines this species is not territorial and pairs will almost nest colonially. Not being territorial it does not need a song to defend its territory and small groups of adults are often seen together in the breeding season. The distinctive 'pinging' note is often the first sign that they are around. Bearded tits are very gregarious at other times of the year, often in small quite mobile flocks. However in winter they become very quiet and tend to move only short distances, foraging low down in the reeds, all their energy devoted to locating food during the short days. However, during frosty spells and especially when snow is on the ground they will resort to the tops of the reeds to feed on the seeds. This is a wonderful sight, but in this exposed position birds are very prone to attacks by sparrowhawks.

Walk number 15

D. Mower

Knot

The knot is usually the most abundant wintering wader in Morecambe Bay. Large flocks occur from October to April with the Lune, Heysham and Walney/Foulney areas being the most favoured localities. The bay is the most important estuary in Britain for this wader with mid-winter counts averaging 66,000. The local fishermen call the knot the 'grey bird', a very apt description of the winter plumage. However the North American name is red knot, which in turn aptly describes the spectacular breeding plumage of reddish chestnut. Birds in this plumage can be seen from late April on and again in August and early September. Amongst a mixed wader flock the knot can be singled out by its intermediate size, larger and more robust than a dunlin, but shorter in the leg than a redshank. In flight knot flocks look much denser than dunlin flocks due to the greater size of the former.

A large flock provides a most spectacular and unforgettable sight. When feeding they form compact flocks giving the impression of a slowly advancing grey carpet. At their roost site on the salt marsh or shingle beach they pack even closer. The spectacle is further heightened when they suddenly take to the wing, twisting and turning at great speed, showing contrasting dark and light colours of the back and under parts while performing intricate aerial manoeuvres rising and descending, quickly gathering in a pack, then thinning out, giving the impression of animated smoke. All this action is accompanied at times by a chorus of excited calling and beating of wings.

The 10–20,000 which gather to roost on the higher spring tides on the helipad at Heysham provide one of the best spectacles, for they are used to people and traffic, so you can enjoy extremely close views as they roost together with large numbers of oystercatchers.

Ringing studies have shown where our wintering knot bred, for there have been 29 ringed birds found in west Greenland and 3 in Arctic Canada.

Walk numbers 1, 2, 3, 6, 7, 10, 12, 13, 16, 18, 22, 23, 24, 26, 27, 29

S. Craig

D. Mower

Bittern

This is another reed bed speciality that is restricted to the Leighton Moss reed beds. The presence of this rare and secretive heron is betrayed by the wonderful 'boom' of the male. This breeding call is part territorial and part attraction; in effect its function is to warn off other males and to attract females! The call, which resembles a foghorn, can be heard over 7 kilometres when all is quiet in the early hours of the morning. They call from late February to early June and the best place to hear them is the public footpath which runs across the centre of Leighton Moss. Early in the booming season the call is more a grunt than a boom, for the oesophagus, which is used as a sounding chamber, is not fully modified and it takes two to three weeks to reach full voice. At the end of the season a similar running down period occurs.

Although the birds mainly keep within the reed cover, at times they fish at the reed edge, especially when the water level is low. Their main prey is eels and other fish, along with frogs, small mammals and freshwater invertebrates. At times they clamber up the reed stems and perch on top of the reeds, quite a feat for such a large bird.

They are also regularly seen in flight when they look more like a large owl than a heron. In May and June when the young are being fed the female makes regular flights between the feeding areas and the nest. Patience is needed but this is usually the easiest time to see this much sought after species. Only the female incubates and feeds the young, whilst the male spends his time booming, attempting to attract other females.

During cold spells the birds often walk on the ice at the waters edge or congregate around the few small areas of open water and this can often be a good time to see them. Because they are such a rare and declining bird, during prolonged cold spells fish are put out to help them survive the harsh conditions.

Reed warbler

S. Craig

As its name suggests this summer visitor is another reed bed speciality. The main population is at Leighton Moss where there are between 3 and 400 pairs, making it the second commonest breeding bird on the reserve after black-headed gull. A few pairs breed in small reed beds near Barrow, Fleetwood and Heysham and at Haweswater near Silverdale. Despite its abundance at Leighton Moss it is not always an easy bird to see, but the male's chattering song readily helps to locate it, and on reasonably calm days it will eventually sidle up to the top of the reed and sing in full view. The song is more repetitive than the sedge warbler's and is also less of a mimic, but at Leighton Moss some have learnt to incorporate bearded tit calls into their song.

The nest is a wonderful work of art, a deep cup made of woven reed strips and other grasses and lined with the previous year's reed flowers and woven round three or four growing reed stems. Occasionally nests are built close to the hides or paths at Leighton Moss and there is much activity when the birds are feeding the young from June to late August. They can be watched quickly threading their way to the nest, the movement of the reeds betraying their silent and invisible presence. The first birds are usually recorded in mid April and although most have left by mid-September a few linger into early October.

Walk numbers 2, 3, 7, 15, 17

D. Mower

Sedge warbler

D. *Mower*

This summer visitor has a wider distribution than its close relative the reed warbler, being more a bird of marshy places, including areas of reed, rush and other waterside vegetation. The largest population is to be found at Leighton Moss; here it occurs all around the edge of the reed bed where reed is giving way to other vegetation. This is a much easier bird to see than the reed warbler for it regularly sings from the tops of a bush from which at times it will launch into a short song flight.

The first birds arrive in mid-April. On arrival the males sing incessantly to attract a mate, but once mated they sing much less. The nest is located low down in a thick tangle of marshy vegetation.

Return migration starts in early August. Just before migrating the birds feed avidly, often on the abundant plum/reed aphids. The bird's normal weight is about 10 grams but just before migration it can weigh up to 18 or 20 grams. It has enough fuel in the form of fat to make quite long migratory flights, possibly as far as south-west France non-stop.

Walk numbers 1, 2, 3, 4, 5, 7, 8, 10, 11, 12, 15, 17, 23, 26, 27, 29

Marsh harrier (*opposite*)

This wonderful marshland raptor is restricted for breeding to Leighton Moss and nearby Haweswater. It is a summer visitor arriving in late March and staying until early September. They first bred in the area as recently 1987 and have increased to a usual population of three or four nests in recent years. On occasions one male may be mated to two females, both of which he brings prey to while they are incubating and while the young are small. They prey on small mammals, frogs and birds, and when the young are in the nest they take many young black-headed gulls. When the male has caught prey it carries it in its feet or talons. When near the nest he calls and the female rises and flies under the male, who drops the prey and she catches it with her talons in flight. This 'food pass' is a most spectacular sight. The parents also use this aerial pass to give food to the flying young but at first the young often fail to catch it and have to retrieve it from the reeds.

When the birds first arrive they have a spectacular 'sky diving display' with the male roller-coasting from a great height and calling to the female. The nest is a platform built deep in the reeds and between two to four young are reared per brood.

Walk numbers 15, 16, 17

Water rail

D. Mower

This is another reed bed speciality, with a breeding population of around 100 pairs at Leighton Moss and small numbers at Haweswater, Cavendish dock, Barrow-in-Furness and Heysham Nature Reserve. This species lives on the floor of the reed bed, its slim build allowing it to walk or swim through the stems searching for freshwater invertebrates, its main food. Because of this it is a very difficult bird to see, but its loud squealing call – more like a pig than a bird and called 'sharming' – betrays its presence throughout the year but especially in spring. The only time it becomes easy to see is during frosty weather when birds leave the cover of the reed bed and congregate around any area of open water. Under such conditions it is not unusual to see up to 30 birds on a walk round the reserve. Smaller numbers can also be seen at other times dashing across the path or flying or swimming across gaps in the reed cover. To see this bird fly more than 25 metres is very unusual but ringing has shown that continental birds winter in our area. A bird ringed at Heysham in winter was found dead near Moscow in Russia, while another one from the Netherlands was found at Leighton Moss.

Walk numbers 3, 4, 8, 10, 15, 17

Reed bunting (*opposite*)

Reed buntings are birds of marshy vegetation, breeding wherever there is sufficient cover. The largest population is at Leighton Moss where the attractively marked males can be seen giving their simple but repetitive song from the tops of the willow bushes or reeds. They are also found nesting on the lower Bowland fells, usually in the thick vegetation surrounding a spring or the meander of a stream. Although they are present throughout the year the bulk of the population moves out of the reed bed and the fell areas and they can be found along the edges of the salt marshes, especially those with thick ungrazed vegetation as at Conder Green. They also frequent weedy arable fields especially on the south of the Lune around Pilling and Cockerham. Ringing has shown that some birds go even further, with recoveries in winter from Dorset and Hampshire. They start to return to the breeding haunts in February.

Walk numbers 1, 2, 3, 4, 5, 6, 7, 8, 9, 10, 11, 12, 13, 15, 17, 18, 19, 22, 23, 24, 26, 27, 29

D. Mower

Coot

The coot is a particularly easy bird to identify, with its unique, bare frontal patch giving rise to the saying 'as bald as a coot'. They are mainly birds of the larger stretches of open fresh water but need some emergent vegetation at the water's edge in which to build their quite large nests. When breeding they are strictly territorial, defending their section of the water's edge with much calling, threat and posture. Rival pairs in dispute patrol with heads low, shoulders hunched and wings raised. At times they fight and all four will lie back in the water and strike each other with their feet, but fights rarely last long. From being so aggressive during the breeding season, by late summer they form large flocks on the deeper, larger areas of open water such as Cavendish dock at Barrow-in-Furness, Hodbarrow and Pine Lake near Carnforth. These also serve as refuge areas during periods of hard frosty weather. Only in very extreme cold spells will they resort to the sea.

Walk numbers 1, 2, 3, 4, 5, 7, 8, 10, 11, 15, 16, 19, 23, 24, 26, 27

S. Craig

Eider

S. Craig

Eiders are large, heavy ducks with a long sloping bill. The breeding population is centred on the South Walney to Foulney part of the bay where they nest in numbers on the ground within the large gull colony. The breeding population in this area has declined somewhat in recent years, although to compensate some have started to breed in other parts of the bay including Chapel Island and a few pairs on the salt marshes on the east of the bay and at Hodbarrow on the Duddon.

Early spring is the best time to see them for the handsome males are intent on their courtship of the rather plain brown females. He gives a wonderful cooing note as he bobs and jerks around the female. Large flocks can be seen at this time off both South Walney and Foulney feeding on the adjacent mussel beds.

In recent winters numbers in the east of the bay between the Wyre and Kent estuaries have increased significantly. Morecambe and Knott End promenades are now excellent places to observe the colourful males and sombre coloured females. In recent years the total wintering population has numbered around 5500 birds.

Walk numbers 1, 2, 3, 6, 10, 12, 13, 16, 18, 22, 23, 24, 26, 27, 29

Teal (*opposite*)

Although a few pairs breed at Leighton Moss this, our smallest duck, is mainly a winter visitor in large numbers to fresh water areas and salt marshes around the bay. Concentrations occur in the Leighton Moss area including the 'Eric Morecambe' complex of pools. It also occurs commonly on the River Lune and at South Walney. Numbers start to build up in late July with the main arrivals from August to early October. In spring numbers will linger well into April. The wintering population within the bay is around 2500.

Ringing has shown that our wintering birds originate from northern Europe. The swift flight of the teal is well known and its ability to rise quickly from the water gives rise to the collective noun for this species of a 'spring of teal'.

For much of the winter and spring, flocks of teal keep up a continuous chorus of a delightful bell-like tinkling call. This is part of the courtship ritual where the male raises himself in the water, quickly raising first the head and then the tail, to display in turn the delicate facial marks and the yellow triangle at the base of the tail. Often several males will display to one apparently uninterested female!

Walk numbers 1, 2, 3, 4, 5, 6, 7, 8, 9, 10, 11, 12, 13, 15, 16, 18, 19, 22, 23, 24, 26, 27, 29

Pintail

S. Craig

This wonderfully elegant and slender duck is a common winter visitor almost exclusively to the coast and estuaries. There are marked concentrations on the Lune estuary near Pilling and on the Keer, Kent, Leven and Duddon estuaries, with a small number inland to Leighton Moss. Except for a few summering non-breeding birds it is a winter visitor with the first birds arriving in late August with further arrivals in September and October. It is a very mobile species with much movement in relation to the tides. Although most birds move out in the late February to March period, numbers can linger well into April. In mid-winter about 3500 have been counted in Morecambe Bay in recent years.

The long neck of this species allows it to feed in somewhat deeper water than the other surface feeding ducks and when upending, the long slim tail is very obvious.

Walk numbers 1, 2, 3, 5, 6, 7, 8, 10, 12, 13, 15, 16, 18, 22, 23, 24, 26, 27, 29

D. Mower

S. *Craig*

Shelduck

One of our commonest ducks which can be seen on the inter-tidal area throughout the year with concentrations on the Lune, Keer, Kent and Leven estuaries. In total about 7000 are counted in mid-winter. At high tide large flocks sit just offshore but at low water they spread out across the sand flats and can be watched sifting through the still wet sand for the marine snail *hydrobia*. For breeding they use rabbit or other holes, a habit which allows the female to be as colourful as the male – no need for camouflage when nesting underground. Most nest within a short distance of the coast but some penetrate inland, especially along the rivers, and nest as far inland as Kirkby Lonsdale. Even during the breeding season large numbers can be seen on the intertidal area; some will be off-duty males but most appear to be immatures or non breeders. Once hatched the young are brought down to the water, often quite a hazardous journey for those nesting well inland.

When the young are around half grown they form large crèches with other broods. These are looked after by a small number of adults while the rest of the population, including all the non-breeding birds, undertake a moult migration which takes them to the Heligoland Bight in Germany. They can be watched setting out on their migration on calm evenings in late July and the Keer estuary is a well known setting off point. The birds become flightless while they renew their flight feathers and they return from early September onward.

Walk numbers 1, 2, 3, 4, 5,6, 7, 8, 9, 10, 11, 12, 13, 14, 15, 16, 17, 18, 19, 22, 23, 24, 26, 27, 29

Gadwall

D. *Mower*

This species is one of the recent success stories of the area. Twenty five years ago it was only regular in small numbers at Leighton Moss, usually no more than ten birds and there were no breeding records. Since then it has increased dramatically with around 20 pairs breeding and an autumn population of up to 200 spread between the meres at Leighton Moss and the Eric Morecambe pools. It is still uncommon elsewhere but it can now turn up almost anywhere in small numbers.

At a distance the rather sombre plumage of the male gadwall is not outstanding but close to in good light it is a wonderful pattern of crescent-shaped grey marks. One good identification feature is the pure white under parts as the bird upends.

Walk numbers 1, 2, 3, 5, 8, 10, 15, 16, 23, 24, 26, 27

Pochard

This is a fresh water diving duck that breeds in small numbers at Leighton Moss and is a winter visitor to most freshwater areas. The largest concentrations in winter are to be found at Cavendish Dock and other reservoirs around Barrow, Hodbarrow, Leighton Moss and Pine Lake near Carnforth. The last two sites share a joint population of about 350 birds. They regularly feed at night on Pine Lake but roost during the day at Leighton Moss.

Walk numbers 1, 2, 3, 4, 5, 7, 8, 10, 15, 16, 19, 23, 24, 26, 27,

D. *Mower*

Twite

S. Craig

This small finch breeds on the moors of the Pennines and in Scotland and is a winter visitor to the area. Flocks arrive in late October and stay until mid-March. Small numbers occur all along the coast but concentrations can be found near Pilling, at Heysham on South Walney and on the salt marshes of the Duddon near Borwick Rails. Recent ringing has revealed that virtually all the wintering birds are drawn from the population breeding in Western Scotland and especially the Inner Hebrides. It has increased as a winter visitor in recent years, possibly because of the changes in Hebridean agriculture, with a move away from arable farming with its associated weed crop to more permanent grassland, so forcing the birds to move south to find winter food. Several of the larger flocks are being encouraged by providing nijer seed which they take to readily, so supplementing their vital winter food.

Walk numbers 1, 2, 3, 7, 10, 12, 13, 22, 23, 24, 26, 27

D. Mower

Common tern

S. Craig

This species may be distinguished from the equally charismatic arctic tern by its longer and lighter coloured red bill with a black tip, longer legs and whiter belly. Sadly, the name common tern belies the current status of this beautiful bird. While it is still a regular summer visitor to the area, breeding status is diminishing on salt marshes and low rocky islands such as Foulney, where it no longer breeds. However, their fickle nature has seen them displaced to major breeding sites elsewhere, including Hodbarrow. Spring passage begins from mid April with small parties heading north into the bay. Throughout the breeding season terns may be seen around the bay and Duddon estuary flying to and from the breeding colonies whilst engaged on fishing forays. The return passage takes place between the end of July and early October. Favoured localities to view an assortment of terns and gulls and test one's identification skills, especially with immatures, include the outfall at Heysham power station.

Walk numbers 1, 2, 3, 4, 5, 6, 7, 8, 10, 13, 16, 18, 19, 22, 23, 24, 26, 27, 29

Black-headed gull (*opposite*)

This is the most familiar of the gulls, well distributed and common throughout the year. There are three breeding colonies within the area. The largest is spread between Leighton Moss and the Eric Morecambe lagoons and is usually around 1500 pairs. Smaller colonies of around 200 pairs each are to be found on Foulney Island and at Hodbarrow. Gulleries are always noisy places with the displays associated with pair formation and nest selection giving way to the constant arrival and departure of incubating or food bearing birds. The nosiest period of all is when the young ones are ready to fly, which is followed by an eerie silence in early July after all have left. Large flocks feed inland throughout the year, although numbers are boosted in winter by immigrants which ringing has shown come from northern Europe, especially from Sweden, Finland and Denmark. Most of these birds roost on the inter-tidal area with roosts spread all around the bay. Here they mingle with other gull species, roosting on the sand flats and floating off when the tide comes in. One of the largest roosts and the easiest to watch assembles each evening off the north end of Morecambe promenade. Gulls come from over Morecambe and there is a marked flight line down the Keer valley.

All walks

Arctic tern

S. Craig

Identification problems distinguishing this species from the similar common tern have led to the term 'comic tern' being applied to doubtful sightings of both species and to probable under-recording. In flight the Arctic tern is easily confused with the common tern but spring birds tend to be much greyer looking, although contrasting with a white under-wing flanked by black tips forming a thin trailing edge along the outer translucent primaries. When perched a telescope view should reveal the Arctic's shorter legs and short dark red bill without a dark tip.

The superbly elegant Arctic tern has earned the name 'sea swallow' and is renowned for travelling vast distances from Antarctica to nest on marshes and remote shingle beaches in northern Europe. During April and May they are commonly seen on spring passage in Morecambe Bay. Return passage peaks during August and September.

Although the species nests sporadically on the Lune marshes, the most important breeding colonies are situated on Foulney Island with 40 breeding pairs in 2005. Local breeding colonies are specially protected, thus birds should never be given cause to dive bomb any human intruder with their distinctive kee-err call.

Walk numbers 1, 2, 3, 5, 6, 8, 10, 12, 13, 16, 18, 22, 23, 24 26, 27, 29

Little tern (*opposite*)

The diminutive little tern is one of the easiest members of the tern family to identify. It is the smallest representative and is best identified by its long angular wings with no tail streamers, and white patch on the forehead contrasting with a black crown, yellow legs and yellow bill with black tip. The butterfly jerky flight and characteristic hover are often accompanied by excited, chattering vocal tones of 'tiri-wiri-tiri-wiri-tiri-wiri', with head held low before plunge-diving into the sea to catch a small fish from a height of 3 to 6 metres.

The little tern is an uncommon summer visitor arriving in mid-April and departing between August and October. Little terns nest in colonies but their main habitat of shingle and sandy beaches round the coast are especially vulnerable being subject to disturbance and are sadly diminishing. Established breeding colonies remain on the Cumbrian coast, particularly at Foulney Island and Hodbarrow, where in a good year a total of around 50 pairs nest.

Walk numbers 24, 26 TO ADD

Sandwich tern

C. Batty

The largest member of the family is named after Sandwich in Kent. It may be distinguished from other terns by a different heavier and whiter looking structure, supporting long grey wings and mantle, short tail fork, black crown and crest and relatively long black bill tipped with yellow.

Sandwich terns arrive back from their winter quarters off the African coast as early as mid to late March. Passage migrants increase during April and flocks are then seen migrating into Morecambe Bay from Fleetwood and Heysham. Sporadic breeding has taken place over many years on the Furness peninsula where up to the 1990s they nested in association with black-headed gulls at Foulney and Walney Islands, but their ephemeral nature has seen them displaced to the major breeding site at Hodbarrow.

From the Millom Iron Works Local Nature Reserve sandwich terns may be observed fishing the Duddon estuary, which is a favoured feeding area for the Hodbarrow colony, with characteristic rasping 'kirrick' call as they plunge into the sea and typically emerge with a sand eel or other tasty morsel.

Walk numbers 1, 2, 3, 6, 7, 10, 12, 16, 18, 22, 23, 24, 26, 27, 29

S. Craig

Leach's petrel

During autumn gales the North West coast is probably the most favoured location in England for observing this charismatic sea bird. The Leach's petrel breeding range extends across the North Atlantic and includes the remotest Hebridean islands of North Rona, St Kilda and the Flannan Isles. Variable numbers occur during sustained September and October westerly gales, providing the only real opportunity to see this species from the shore. During suitable conditions Leach's petrel may be seen off Rossall Point, Fleetwood, Heysham and Walney Island. Storm driven birds or 'wrecks' occasionally reach double figures along the coast, and on occasions are predated by the larger gulls. Exceptionally storm driven individuals also occur on inland waters such as Leighton Moss.

For this species the precise wind direction is a crucial local consideration, and what is right for Rossall Point may not be right for other Leach's hotspots such as Walney Island. Character or jizz is important in separating Leach's from the similar storm petrel. To witness a diminutive dark brown Leach's petrel battling against the elements of a horrendous sea pattering just above the breakers, with buoyant tern-like flight on long-angled, pointed wings contrasting with a white rump above a notched tail, is a real ornithological challenge and memorable experience – long may it remain so!

Walk numbers 1, 3, 6, 12, 13, 16, 18, 22, 24, 26, 29

Leaches petrel

S. *Craig*

Gannet

The adult gannet or solan goose is unmistakeable and is our largest sea bird. This superb cigar-shaped sea bird with narrow wings is a truly marine species designed for the rigours of the ocean and comes ashore only to nest in vast colonies, at traditional sites mainly on rocky islands, the nearest colonies being Scar Rocks, south west Scotland.

Spring passage begins at the end of March and small numbers may be seen during the summer. The return passage of adults and immatures, often flying in a single line, peaks during August and extends until October. There are several successive phases of immature plumage and the species does not attain adult plumage until around five years of age. Gannets are rarely seen in winter when their range extends south to the coast of west Africa and the Atlantic islands.

Sightings of gannet, often having been driven in by storms, are possible in favoured coastal locations off Blackpool and Heysham. The largest numbers can be seen off Walney, Hodbarrow and Silecroft where the spectacle of large numbers of gannets diving vertically into the sea in pursuit of shoals of mackerel is a bird watching highlight.

Walk numbers 1, 3, 13, 16, 18, 22, 24, 26, 27, 29

S. Craig

Lapwing

This attractive wader with its bizarre tall crest, rounded wings, glossy green back and rich chestnut patches above and below the tail is easily identified. It is still fairly widely distributed as a resident breeding bird on the major nature reserves but unfortunately has suffered severe declines due to agricultural intensification and regular silage cutting. It is a passage migrant and abundant winter visitor to the mudflats and estuaries of Morecambe Bay.

Arriving on the breeding grounds during the first mild spell of late winter, the males establish their territories with erratic aerial dances accompanied by excited bouts of calling. The male attracts the female by scraping a hollow in frenzied haste and bending forward with his breast to the ground while sporting his rich chestnut tail patches to entrance the female. Both sexes share incubation and care of the young.

Flocking starts in late June and most have left the breeding grounds by early July to congregate in large flocks in lowland areas adjacent to the coastline. Numbers are supplemented during the autumn and winter, particularly during periods of hard frost. Ringing has shown that many of these birds originate from Scandinavian countries.

All walks

Curlew

This unmistakable wader with its six-inch long, de-curved bill and bulky brown body is a resident, winter visitor and passage migrant. There are several local ringing recoveries indicating birds of Finnish origin.

Resident birds do not have to journey very far between the winter feeding grounds and breeding areas such as those in Bowland. From late February through to July it is the characteristic bird of the moors and farmland that surround the bay. The evocative wild liquid bubbling call of the curlew is one of the most evocative and familiar sounds in nature and the beautiful whistle has given the species its name. The sharp, repeated alarm call warns of danger and as the nesting season progresses the sentinel of the pair will, on detecting danger, alert its incubating mate with frantic calls. After the young are hatched the pair will attempt to courageously drive off any predators.

The curlew is an abundant winter visitor and is widely distributed around the bay, with a five year average of 12,500 birds making this the most important estuary for the species in Britain.

All walks

S. *Craig*

Herring and lesser black-backed gulls

S. Craig

Both these two closely related species nest side by side in large mixed breeding colonies on South Walney Nature Reserve and on the Bowland Fells at Tarnbrook and for expediency are dealt with together. The lesser black-backed gull is now a resident breeding bird and passage migrant. It used to be almost exclusively a summer visitor but in recent years increasing numbers have wintered around the bay, depending on easy pickings on landfill sites. The herring gull is an abundant winter visitor, passage migrant and common resident.

Both species are back on territory at South Walney and Tarnbrook during the first mild spell of late winter. The Tarnbrook mixed colony is the largest inland gull colony in Britain. During the early 1980s it was considered that there may have been up to 30,000 pairs but numbers have declined to less than a third of this in recent years partly due to efforts to cull them to protect water catchment interests. There are now approximately 7,000 breeding pairs of lesser black-backed gulls that greatly outnumber the herring gulls at less than 500 pairs.

Significantly there is a continual passage of birds to and from Tarnbrook to Morecambe Bay and the Lancashire coast where they collect much of their food. By contrast to Tarnbrook the South Walney colony utilises the shore and coastal sand dunes for nesting. Here the largest ground nesting gull colony in Europe was estimated in 2000 at 22,000 lesser black-backed and 9500 herring gulls.

Territories are vacated during August and both species remain in the bay throughout the autumn and winter.

All walks

S. Craig

S. *Craig*

Kittiwake

The kittiwake is a remarkably gentle and attractive looking gull of grey and white plumage with pale yellow bill and distinctive black legs and wing tips. Immature kittiwakes or tarrochs have a black band at the base of the tail and neck and a distinctive diagonal black band across the wings.

The kittiwake is a fairly common passage migrant and winter visitor to Morecambe Bay especially during March, April, September and October. They are usually seen off Fleetwood, Heysham and the Cumbrian coast when squally conditions and westerly onshore winds bring them near the coast. Kittiwakes are less commonly observed during June and July whilst they are occupied at the nearest principal breeding colonies located at St Bee's Head, Cumbria and the North Wales coast. However, the first recorded nesting of the species around Morecambe Bay took place in 1998 when two pairs bred on a gas platform in the Morecambe Bay central field. This colony increased to 22 pairs in 2002 and significantly this particular offshore installation was the first to host a nesting bird in U.K. waters.

Walk numbers 1, 2, 3, 13, 16, 18, 22, 23, 24, 26, 27, 29

S. Craig

Great black-backed gull

This is the largest of the commoner British breeding gulls and may be distinguished from the similar lesser black-backed gull by its much darker mantle, pale pink legs and heavier frame. The great black-backed gull is a common winter visitor and passage migrant and nests in small numbers. High cliffs and headlands are the preferred breeding site such as those on rocky islands in Wales and Scotland. Around Morecambe Bay this habitat is lacking and the species has adapted to ground nesting. The main population is at South Walney where 80 pairs were counted in 2000 and there are around ten pairs on the Bowland fells at Tarnbrook. Sporadic nesting has also occurred elsewhere, including at Leighton Moss and on the roofs of the BAE Systems complex at Barrow-in-Furness.

Winter populations gather where coastal feeding opportunities exist. They are a familiar sight among flocks of gulls that gather on rubbish tips and on the sands of the bay, especially in estuarine locations between November and the end of January. On North Walney Island around 300 birds occur at established roost sites.

Walk numbers 1, 2, 3, 5, 6, 7, 8, 12, 13, 15, 16, 17, 18, 19, 22, 23, 24, 26, 27, 29

Bar-tailed godwit

The bar-tailed godwit is a winter visitor and passage migrant from the tundra regions of Norway, Finland and North Russia to favoured coastal localities. These include the sands and inter tidal mud creeks of the Fylde coast, Wyre and Lune estuaries and Walney Island. Peak numbers are seen from October to March but recent surveys illustrate that during the last five years the bay population has declined from around 7,000 to 5000 birds.

Although rarely seen in summer plumage, the males are superbly handsome with wholly rusty red under parts. During winter some confusion may arise in distinguishing bar-tailed from the similar black-tailed godwit. The bar-tailed is smaller and rather dumpy, standing less tall with a shorter neck and legs and slightly upturned bill. Not surprisingly it has a barred grey tail instead of a black one but this feature is not always easy to observe. In flight it may be distinguished from the black-tailed godwit by the lack of the distinctive white wing bar of the latter and on jizz: bar-tailed flocks fly fast and direct, cascading down onto the sands where they run about at the tide edge in excited, hurried groups.

Walk numbers 1, 3, 6, 7, 12, 13, 18, 22, 24, 26, 29

S. Craig

S. Craig

Red-throated diver

The red-throated diver is a fairly common winter visitor and spring passage migrant to Morecambe Bay and the Duddon estuary. Variable numbers occur offshore from September but with increased northward passage during the period February to April. They may be observed at regular watched localities such as those at Rossall Point, Heysham, Morecambe Stone Jetty, Jenny Brown's Point, South Walney and Silecroft beach. Summer plumage is unmistakeable but in winter the smaller and paler red-throated diver may be distinguished from the black-throated and great northern diver by the distinctive outline of the slightly upturned bill; a feature that is also recognisable in flight together with the distinctive hump back and plain wings.

Walk numbers 1, 2, 3, 6, 10, 12, 13, 16, 18, 22, 23, 24, 26, 27, 29

Grey heron (*opposite*)

The grey heron is an unmistakeable breeding resident, passage migrant and winter visitor to Morecambe Bay. Favoured haunts include shallow tidal waters and estuarine marshes and mudflats at the channel edge, and inland rivers, streams, ponds and lakes. The meres at Leighton Moss provide classic habitat and here fishing herons are fascinating to watch as they wade stealthily with their eyes focussed along the bill, waiting for an opportunity to stab a prize catch with tremendous accuracy and speed.

Herons are subject to population crashes during prolonged hard winters such as the freezing conditions experienced during the severe winter of 1962/63. Since then national and local populations have prospered, probably as a result of the continuing trend for fairly mild winters. In late winter birds start to gather on what is termed 'standing grounds'. These are close to the breeding colony and at the Dallam heronry by late February 40 to 60 birds can be seen on the sand flats of the Kent estuary.

Breeding takes place at established heronries close to the coastal plain, with herons travelling considerable distances for food to sustain their growing family in their tree top nests. The most important heronries are on private estates at Dallam Towers, Milnthorpe, Causeway End near Back Barrow and Claughton-on-Brock, where breeding populations have seen fluctuations but remain fairly stable.

All walks

D. Mower

S. *Craig*

Greenshank

The greenshank is a regular passage migrant to Morecambe Bay, especially during the mid July to October period, but is less common in spring on northward migration; a few occasionally over-winter. As a summer visitor to Britain it breeds in the remotest highlands and islands of Scotland and Scandinavia. When the breeding season ends small parties move to the coast to commence their long migration to Africa. In late summer the greenshank is a regular passage migrant to the gravel pools and Lighthouse Bay at South Walney where there are records throughout the year. At Leighton Moss Reserves the reed-fringed muddy edges are favoured but it is the Eric Morecambe complex that consistently sustains large flocks of up to 40 birds during peak late summer migration and offers the best viewing conditions around Morecambe Bay.

Greenshank are often seen in association with the commoner redshank. It may be distinguished from the redshank by its larger size, greyer mantle, contrasting white under parts and head, green bill and green legs. It has a distinctive call – 'kyu kyu kyu' – that is usually given by an alarmed bird taking to the air. In flight it displays a plain wing bar and white rump.

Walk numbers 1, 2, 3, 6, 7, 8, 10, 12, 13, 15, 16, 18, 22, 23, 24, 26, 27, 29

Sunderland Point

Knot

Walk 12A

Start: Potts Corner car park at the end of Carr Road, Middleton
Grid reference: SD 413572
Distance: 5 km (3.1 miles)
Time: Allow 4 to 5 hours
Grade: Easy
General: Toilets at Sunderland Point village by car park. Refreshments at Pots Corner or Overton

THIS IS ONE OF THE BEST YEAR-ROUND birding areas on Morecambe Bay. Not only does it have one of the largest high tide wader roosts on spring tides but it is also an excellent area on both the lower tides and at low water. Because the start points differ depending on the tide heights the walks are described separately. It is vital not to park at Sunderland Point itself on anything but the lowest tides as the parking area is covered on most tides. Walk 12A is best done on tides above 9.2m (Liverpool height) and it is recommended to start the walk at least two hours before high tide.

1. *Park in the Potts Corner car park (charges may apply at certain times) and set out on the track which heads along the tide-line to Sunderland Point.*

From the car park check the foreshore to the right to see if waders are starting to assemble. Most waders come in from the north so it is well worth checking occasionally to watch the build up of the flocks on the inter-tidal area. The track passes through salt marsh which is good for meadow and rock pipits,

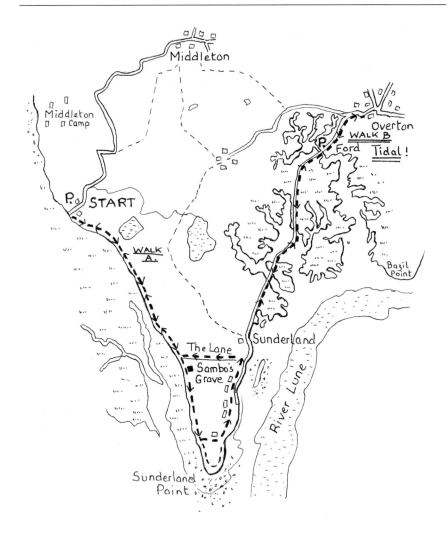

skylarks and pied, and in spring, white wagtails. Snipe are regularly flushed and at times jack snipe, although to flush the snipe, which only takes off at the last moment, you will need to deviate from the track onto the salt marsh – wellingtons are recommended! The tide-line with its scattered bushes often holds flocks of finches, especially in late summer when good numbers of linnets, greenfinch and reed buntings can be seen. The bushes also hold migrant warblers in season, while the hedgerows with a thick undergrowth of reed often produce stonechats and the fields are well worth checking for curlew, lapwing and at certain times golden plover.

Close to the farm and just behind the high tide mark there is a small fresh-water pool and field well used by cattle. This occasionally attracts wildfowl, once even a long-tailed duck, but there are usually many pied wagtails and meadow pipits and the occasional grey wagtails and some finches. Choose a good vantage point opposite the gathering waders and watch as the flocks of oystercatcher, curlew, knot, dunlin, redshank and grey plover gather. With them are smaller numbers of bar-tailed godwit, ringed plover and sanderling. Numbers, and to some extent variety, change with the seasons. At passage times this is the best area for whimbrel and greenshank. The sudden panic of the smaller waders usually signals the presence of potential predators, usually peregrine, merlin or sparrowhawk. In winter short-eared owls also frequent this marsh. They are day time hunters but spend a lot of time hidden in thick cover, but if the marsh floods they take flight into the fields where they will sit on fence posts giving excellent views. Wildfowl are mainly shelduck, wigeon, teal and mallard. Cormorants are regular, often sitting on the anti-invasion posts on the now covered sand flats.

2. *Continue along the tide-line past Sambo's grave to the end of the point. Spring tides in the bay occur around midday so the end of the point is a good lunch spot. Here you can watch both the bay and the Lune channel.*

If you time it carefully you should arrive here just after high tide and you can watch the wader roost start to break up as the waders return to feed. The stones just in front of you often attract the first birds, usually turnstone, grey plover and ringed plover. In May and very early June this is an excellent place to see the spring passage of numbers of sanderling, many in full summer plumage, and ringed plover. These migrants are heading for their breeding grounds in Iceland and in the case of the sanderling, Greenland. The Lune channel regularly has mergansers, goldeneye, great crested grebe and, especially in late summer and early autumn, common, sandwich and occasionally little terns pass up and down the channel. Further ebbing of the tide produces more waders, some of which cross the Lune towards Cockersands lighthouse but most head out following the quickly receding tide with the smaller waders leaving first, followed by the larger oystercatcher and curlew.

3. *Follow the tide-line past the picturesque Sunderland Hall (dating from 1683) and on towards the small village of Sunderland Point, then up onto the narrow road in front of the houses. Depending on where birds are, there should be several stops before you reach the end of the village and the small informal car park and toilets.*

Looking at today's tranquil scene with a scattering of small boats at anchor, it is hard to believe that Sunderland Point three hundred years ago was a hive of industry. Alongside the still surviving stone jetty, ships would be unloading their cargos of cotton and sugar from Jamaica or Barbados. The dark side of this trade, of course, was its association with the slave trade. African slaves were captured and taken to the West Indies in exchange for cotton and sugar. Others ships would bring tar from Norway or trade with Ireland and the Isle of Man. Boats were also built or fitted out here and many of the present houses started life as warehouses serving this trade, as did the two pubs and lodging houses. In latter years Sunderland Point became a fashionable sea-bathing venue.

With a quickly falling tide the sand banks and mussel beds attract good numbers of waders and gulls. Besides the wader species which were listed at the roost site these areas often attract large flocks of golden plover and, usually on the far side of the river, black-tailed godwit. At passage times check the dunlin flocks for curlew, sandpipers, little stints and sanderling, while the muddy creeks are also good for spotted redshank and whimbrel. The stony mussel skeers are an excellent place to watch how turnstones got their name. Terns often perch with the more abundant gulls, of which in winter there are usually the five common species but glaucous and Mediterranean have also occurred. Further up the channel flocks of wigeon, mallard sheiduck and teal along with good numbers of mute swans are regular, along with smaller numbers of eider, merganser and goldeneye. From late spring onwards the Lune channel is a favourite nursery area for sheiduck, with broods gradually being amalgamated in large crèches as most of the adults leave on their moult migration in late July, leaving just a few adults behind in charge of the young. The adults migrate to the Heligoland Bight in Germany to moult, and return in September resplendent in their new feathers.

4. *If you have time you can continue along the road for a distance before retracing your steps to the centre of the village (the birds you are likely to see are included in Walk B below). Take the lane that runs right across the peninsula and this will take you to the outer side of the point and so rejoin the track back to the car park.*

Round the houses are the usual garden birds and up to at least mid-September breeding house martins. After passing the last house look over the stone wall to the right to a small pool close by in the field, as at any time of year it may just hold moorhens but it really comes into its own in summer during a dry spell. A constant passage of birds settling to drink may be seen, including many linnets, goldfinches, wagtails and pipits, while in the bushes at the back of the pool willow warblers and whitethroats join the resident tits. It is also worth scanning the fields where little owls are regularly seen, often perching on fence posts. The more distant lower lying fields often hold flocks of feeding lapwing and golden plover and in winter redwing and fieldfare.

Bar-tailed godwit

Walk 12B: An Evening Saunter to Sunderland

Snipe

Start: Informal car park just out of Overton on the
Sunderland Point road
Grid reference: SD432576
Distance: 2.5 km (1.6 miles)
Time: Allow 2 to 3 hours
Grade: Easy

THIS SHORT WALK IS PROBABLY BEST done as an evening walk from late July
to September as the evening tides are always low, although it can be done
as a low water walk. It is absolutely imperative that you check the tide height
and time before setting out – tides above 8.5 m can flood the road!

1. *Park in the small informal car park just past the up and over on the Overton to
Sunderland Point road and walk along the road towards Sunderland Point, scanning
the salt marsh and tidal creeks.*

The birds to be seen in late summer are described here. Low water sightings
at other times of the year will be similar but of course the summer visitors
and passage birds will be absent. Significant flocks of curlew and lapwing
regularly roost on the salt marsh, so check the curlew flocks for the
diminutive whimbrel, although the first clue that the bird is about is its
distinctive 'seven whistler' call. The road passes close to the sea wall in
places and it is well worth checking the fence posts for little owls or the
wires for flocks of linnets, which regularly feed along the tide-line and out
onto the salt marsh. Flocks of skylarks and meadow pipits also frequent the
higher salt marsh.

The road passes over several tidal creeks which are well used by feeding
redshank, dunlin, turnstone and ringed plover. The most productive creeks
are the larger ones toward Sunderland Point. Here also there are large areas

of exposed sand between the creeks, and the main channel of the Lune comes into view. In late summer this is a real wader hot spot. It is well worth searching through the large mixed flocks of small waders, numbers of which depend on the state of the tide, the largest numbers usually occurring on a falling tide. In good years numbers of curlew, sandpipers, little stints, ruff and sanderling mix in with the abundant dunlin, redshank and ringed plover. Several rarer waders have also occurred. The gradually exposing rocky skears are patronised by large flocks of golden plover and lapwing. With them are smaller numbers of turnstone, many of which in late summer will have just returned from their Arctic breeding grounds. They are resplendent in full breeding plumage, as are some of the knot and bar-tailed godwit which usually only occur in smaller numbers.

Many birds pass up and down the river, including both Arctic and common terns from the small colony further up the river. A motley collection of five species of gull is always present, many of them in the dull grey-brown plumage of birds of the year which are gradually moving away from their natal colonies. Wildfowl include many shelduck; early in the summer almost all are the rather washed out juveniles but by September many adult birds will have returned in fresh plumage from the moulting grounds. Recently eiders have become regular, easy to spot because of their large bulk. The first winter wildfowl will also be present, usually wigeon and possibly pintail.

Kestrel

2. *Walk as far as time and light conditions allow, remembering of course that you have to walk back to your car so allow plenty of time for this as the birds will no doubt have changed, attracting your attention again.*

Heysham Nature Reserve and Heysham Harbour Area

On both of thee walks it is possible to include a visit to the Lancashire Wildlife Trust Nature reserve at Heysham Power Station and the harbour area. On mid day spring tides there is plenty of time to visit the nature reserve before setting out on the walk from Potts corner at Middleton. Access is gained by following the signs to Heysham harbour, taking the A589 for 1 mile before turning left at the traffic lights at Moneyclose Lane. The reserve entrance is 200 metres on the right hand side. Details of access to the sea watching hide overlooking the power station outfalls are posted at the hut by the car park, where a reserve guide is also available. Enquire at the Visitor Centre about access to the other sites in the area and up to date bird news. Grid Reference SD407601. Website; www.lancswt.org.uk

The reserve has a good range of breeding scrub and marshland birds including lesser whitethroat, whitethroat and sedge warbler. It has an impressive list of rarities many of which are attracted in by the 'lighthouse' effect of the power station's floodlights. These have included bee-eater, serin, woodchat, shrike and at least 10 yellow-browed warblers. Butterflies include small skipper, grayling and gatekeeper along with 14 species of dragonfly.

The sea watching hide is well worth a visit especially during passage periods with strong westerly winds. Indeed the sea wall on both sides of the harbour entrance is one of the best sea watching sites on the Bay. Specialities include skuas, auks, petrels and shags. Terns and sea birds are also attracted in by the ever moving water of the outfalls. the Red Rocks close to the sea watching hide attract roosting waders including turnstone along with a small flock of wigeon. The helipad situated close to the north harbour wall attracts a large roost of knot and oystercatcher on the highest Spring tides.

Heysham Flash: A former Lancashire wetland site which is now occupied by Heysham power station (photo D. Hindle)

Morecambe to Bolton-Le-Sands

Turnstone.

Start: Morecambe stone jetty
Grid reference: SD426647
Distance: 7 km (4.3 miles)
Time: Allow 4 to 5 hours
Grade: Easy
General: Toilets at Hest Bank on seaward side of level crossing and at Bolton-le-Sands behind the sea wall near Red Bank Farm. Refreshments at Hest Bank

Wheelchair access to stone jetty and Morecambe promenade at the car park across the level crossing at Hest Bank

MORECAMBE PROMENADE IS ONE OF THE BEST bird watching sites around the bay and there is always something to see throughout the year and at any state of the tide. However, the best bird watching occurs between late August through to late May, on days when the tide is higher than 8.5 metres (Liverpool height). Tides between 9 and 9.7 metres are the best for they allow more time to cover the whole walk as the tide ebbs and flows. Tides higher than this occur only usually at the spring and autumn equinoxes and are best avoided as the salt marshes and groynes are covered and the waders flight to the large salt marsh to the north of the Keer estuary.

This is a one way walk, and return to the start is easily accomplished on the regular Carnforth to Morecambe bus service which you can join at Bolton-le-Sands, although if you need the exercise it is of course possible to walk back and view the birds at low water.

1. *There are adequate parking facilities close to the Morecambe stone jetty where it is best to park around two and a half hours before high tide. Walk to the end of the jetty.*

On approaching the jetty check the gulls that frequent the prom. A few Mediterranean gulls are regular here and some of them will take bread, allowing a close inspection. Several of them are colour ringed and a close study over the years has revealed that the wintering birds are drawn from as far away as Poland and the Czech Republic – one bird from Poland has been coming for at least nine years. With much sand still exposed there is usually a good selection of waders visible from the jetty, including oystercatcher, dunlin, knot, redshank and bar-tailed godwit. These will move off as the tide begins to flow. The attention then shifts to the water close to the end of the jetty where there are usually numbers of merganser, eider and goldeneye. Further out there may be numbers of great crested grebe along with small numbers of red-throated diver and common scoter and possibly guillemot. If the wind is reasonably strong from a westerly direction there may be a passage of gannet, and in spring and autumn, sandwich, common and Arctic terns and possibly skuas. To allow time to see the Hest Bank wader roost at its best, leave the jetty at least one and a half hours before high tide.

2. *Returning to the promenade walk north on the prom past the Eric Morecambe statue (Eric is sporting a pair of binoculars!) until you come to the first of two rock-armoured groynes just past Morecambe town hall. These are part of the recent strengthening of the sea defences.*

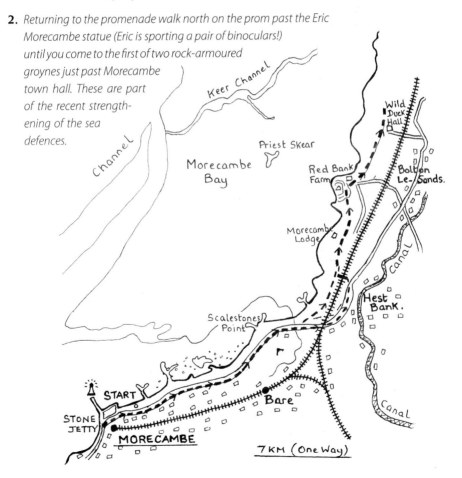

In this section continue to check the many larger gulls which perch on the rocks or sit on the sea. Most will be lesser black-backed or herring gulls but check for Mediterranean gulls. Out to sea there will be an almost continual movement of waders as the tide displaces them. The first rock groyne provides a secure roosting site on all but the highest tides for many oyster-catchers, redshank and turnstone, and at passage times common and Arctic terns. Cormorants also use the breakwater and any adjoining towers, often standing with their wings hanging out to dry. Goldeneye, shelduck eider and great crested grebe regularly pass the tide on the sea. The second groyne is lower but is used by many waders, including knot and dunlin on the lower tides and as a gathering point on the higher tides before it is covered. At low water the area between the two groynes supports a mussel bed which is a favourite feeding area for many waders.

3. *Continue along the promenade to the end until you come to the VVV leisure complex.*

Along this section of the route more wildfowl start to appear, especially wigeon, shelduck and pintail, and in some winters a small flock of scaup occurs. Great crested grebes are usually further out, with the occasional common scoter or possibly the much rarer long-tailed duck. A good vantage point is opposite the final groyne, where waders and gulls often roost, especially on the lower tides. Besides the typical coastal waders there are often numbers of lapwing and a few golden plover. If the tide is still flowing waders will continue to arrive from the feeding areas as the food-rich sand flats become covered. The differences between the times of arrival at the roost are closely related to the food that each species takes and where that food is to be found on the sand flats. The two extremes are oystercatcher and ringed plover.

Curlew N.B.

Oystercatchers feed on the mussel and cockle beds which occur on the lower parts of the tidal cycle and are covered first by the tide, so they usually stop feeding around two hours before high tide. By contrast, ringed plover feed on the snail *hydrobia* and the sandhopper *corophium*, both of which occur on the higher sand banks so often they can feed right up to high tide. (See introduction for more details.)

4. *On the lower tides it is possible to walk along the bottom of the railway embankment on the rocks and shingle and then on to the road on the sea wall that starts at the level crossing. On higher tides it is safer to return to the end of the promenade and follow the main road to the Hest Bank level crossing, where you can cross the railway by the* *footbridge. The elevation provides an excellent place for an overall view of the salt marsh with its large wader roost. Once on the embankment and road at the back of the salt marsh the best view point depends on where the waders eventually settle. There is usually some segregation of the species so it is best to move slowly along the embankment to get the best view.* **Do not venture out onto the salt marsh**.

Large numbers of oystercatcher, dunlin, knot, redshank and curlew are usually present, with smaller numbers of bar-tailed godwit, turnstone and ringed plover, though numbers change throughout the year and with the height of the tide. For example, the largest numbers of ringed plover occur in late summer and especially in late April and May. The largest numbers of turnstone occur when the groynes further down the promenade are covered or disturbed. While the tide continues to flow there is much movement of the waders as their roost sites are flooded and they are pushed onto an even smaller area of salt marsh. The time of high tide is usually easy to detect for the waders suddenly become settled and calm descends on the assembled multitudes. This can of course be quickly shattered by the sudden appearance of a merlin and especially a peregrine, which provoke panic in the massed ranks of the smaller waders. This is a magnificent spectacle as the waders weave and turn at great speed and the predator tries to out fly or stoop on its intended prey. You may wonder how they could miss with so many birds to choose from but, although they are often successful, they also regularly leave empty clawed! On occasion after repeated stoops the wader flocks are pressurised to move to an alternative site.

Wildfowl include numbers of wigeon which graze on the salt marsh turf, many shelduck which usually sit out on the water, and varying numbers of pintail and shoveler. Check the old tide-lines for wintering rock pipits and at passage periods, meadow pipits, pied and white wagtails and wheatears.

5. *The route continues along the back of the salt marsh towards Bolton-le-Sands and the eroded headland of Red Bank. There is a signed public footpath over the small hill of Red Bank which allows good views across the bay and returns to the salt marsh track at Red Bank Farm. There is also a path along the back of the salt marsh among the rocks of the bank. The embankment and coastal path eventually lead to the road to Bolton-le-Sands, the A6 and the bus route. If times allows and the tide is still in, a short walk of around 75 metres along the road on the seaward side of Wild Duck Hall is recommended before turning back to go down Mill Lane to the A6.*

The Red Bank area occasionally has small flocks of wintering twite and black redstarts have wintered there also. The Bolton-le-Sands Marsh holds the largest numbers of wildfowl along this section of the bay especially at the northern end near the aptly named Wild Duck Hall. They mainly congregate along the salt marsh edge at high tide and include numbers of wigeon, pintail, mallard, shoveler and teal.

Warton Crag

Peregrine

N.B.

Start: Starts and finishes in the main Warton Crag
Quarry car park

Grid reference: SD491723

Distance: 3 km (1.9 miles)

Time: Allow 2 to 3 hours

Grade: Moderate

General: Toilets and other facilities in Warton village

THIS SHORT WALK COVERS ONE OF THE MOST interesting limestone outcrops or crags in the Morecambe Bay area. It gives a quite sharp climb to the summit through areas of limestone grassland and scrub. The walk commences within the huge Warton Crag Quarry Nature Reserve managed by Lancashire County Council. Indeed the whole of Warton Crag is a nature reserve administered jointly by Lancaster City Council, Lancashire County Council, Lancashire Wildlife Trust and the RSPB, who each are responsible for their separate sections.

The massive disused quarry is now weathering and vegetating. It is the well known breeding site of peregrine and raven along with a large colony of jackdaws and a pair of kestrels. Superb views of all these can be obtained from the car park. These birds are in residence usually from February to July and all four species use the quarry as a roost or daytime resting site at other times of the year so it is well worth checking the cliffs on arrival. Both barn and little owls have also been seen on the cliff in recent years. Spare a little time to reflect that all the limestone excavated to produce this huge quarry was transported along the steep narrow road through Warton. Details of the history of the quarry and its geology can be found on the display boards in the car park.

1. *From the quarry go out of the car park onto the road and turn right up the hill as far as the gate to the RSPB reserve. Follow the track through a second gate then a stile and take the path to the right that eventually reaches the summit. There is a rather confusing maze of paths in some areas and for bird watching it is best to explore some of these. It really is impossible to get lost if you make for the summit.*

↑ Leighton Moss

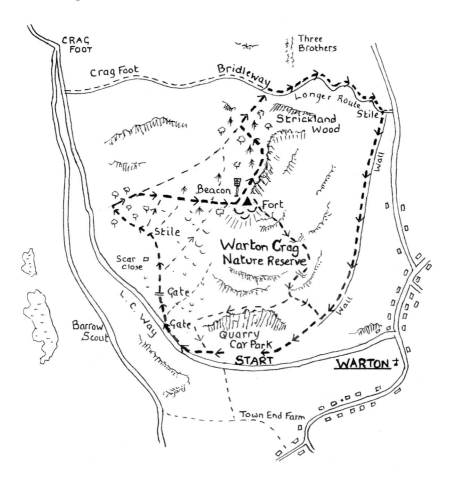

The scrub and patches of more mature trees support a good range of breeding warblers, with willow warbler and garden warbler the most abundant, followed by blackcap, chiffchaff, whitethroat and lesser whitethroat. Among the residents are marsh tit, long-tail tit, bullfinch and both great spotted and green woodpeckers. The latter can regularly be seen feeding on ants on the limestone grassland. One apparently bizarre sight in this very dry habitat is groups of displaying shelduck that nest in holes in the limestone. Even mallard have been found nesting close to the summit, though removing the young down to the distant wetland areas must be quite a task.

An evening visit from late March to late June can be very rewarding as this is one of the best sites in the area for watching woodcock undertake their evening 'roding' flight. The fast, jerky wing beats of the male with its strange grunting and squeaking call are all part of the territorial display. Although they can be seen at times from most parts of the crag, the best site is in the glade around 50 metres the other side of the stile. The glade allows long views and, on occasions, up to four birds have been seen in the air at once.

Pick a reasonably calm evening and set out about an hour before sunset. The views across Morecambe Bay and over to the Lakeland fells are stunning and the sunsets superb. To the east stretch the Pennines with Ingleborough the most striking feature. As darkness approaches the evening chorus of blackbird, song thrush and robin is joined by the distinctive hoot of the resident tawny, further heightening an all round atmospheric experience. Many years ago nightjars occurred regularly in this area but they have not been recorded since the 1960s. However with the recent increase in some parts of the country there is always the possibility that they may return, so it is well worth listening out for their unmistakeable churring song in late spring and summer although, when present, they start to call quite a bit later in the evening than woodcock.

Although spring is certainly the most productive time to visit, autumn can also be rewarding. In most years flocks of goldfinches and smaller numbers of siskin and redpoll feed on the abundant knapweed and other seeds. In a good berry year large numbers of redwing and fieldfare stay until the crop of hawthorn berries is exhausted. Buzzard and raven are regular throughout the year. At migration times the crag is a good watch point, especially for raptors and osprey, red kite and hen, whilst marsh harrier have been recorded recently.

The summit was used as a hill fort by the Brigantes in pre-Roman times, while the caves of the crag were well used by early man, as the tools and weapons now in the British museum prove. What a commanding position they chose, with the marshes and the sea to give further protection. For centuries the summit has been used as a beacon when messages had to be flashed across the country. The present beacon was erected as part of the last celebration of the anniversary of the defeat of the Spanish Armada.

2. *From the summit take the path that is close to the summit escarpment then descend into the ash and birch woodland on the east flank of the crag. Again there is a network of paths but all eventually lead to the main path down. Return to the car park on the path that runs alongside the roadside wall.*

The resident breeding birds within the more mature woodland are predominantly titmice with smaller numbers of treecreeper, nuthatch, great spotted and green woodpeckers.

Warton crag is a prime site for the all-round naturalist. Botanically it has a diverse limestone flora both within the woodlands and on the grasslands. The deeper loess soils are acidic, allowing for further diversity. Among the more striking woodland plants are wonderful carpets of bluebells and ransoms in spring. On the limestone grassland birds-foot trefoil, rock rose, primrose, cowslip and hawk bits are abundant. A careful search will reveal milkwort and eyebright and on the limestone pavement lily of the valley. Orchids include swathes of early purple and smaller numbers of common spotted and a local limestone speciality, dark red helleborine.

Two plants especially attractive to nectaring butterflies are knapweed and marsh thistle. Twenty two species of butterfly are regular. To locate them, the flight season and their habitat preferences must be taken into account. Dingy skipper, green hairstreak, northern brown argus, wall and grayling favour the limestone grassland areas. The specialities are the pearl, small pearl and high brown fritillaries for which the best area is the ride recommended for watching woodcock. The food plants of the caterpillars of all three fritillaries are the abundant violets.

Leaflets about the Warton Crag Nature Reserve and the Iron Age Hill Fort are available from the Arnside/Silverdale AONB Unit who can be contacted at info@arnsidesilverdaleaonb.org.uk

Wintry scene on Warton Crag (photo by D. Hindle)

Leighton Moss RSPB Reserve

Bearded Reedling   C.D.

Start: Starts and returns to the Leighton Moss car
park and visitor centre
Grid reference: SD477749
Distance: 6 km (3.7 miles)
Time: Any time from 3 to 9 hours
Grade: Easy
General: Toilets, tea-room and shop at the
visitor centre
♿ Wheelchair access to four hides, shop and
display area. Chair lift to tea room

Leighton Moss is one of the North West's best year-round bird watching
sites with an excellent range of reed bed, wetland and woodland birds, all
viewable from superb facilities set in glorious restful scenery, provided by the
backdrop of limestone woodland, heath and rolling farmland.

1. *Park in the car park by the visitor centre. If arriving after 09.30 obtain your permit and
reserve guide and map from the visitor centre. Leighton Moss is very accessible by public
transport, both bus and rail, and to encourage this environmentally friendly mode of
travel, free access is given on production of a valid bus or rail ticket.*

An earlier start is possible as the public hide and footpath is open at all
times and the rest of the reserve at 09.00 until dusk, and this is the recommended route for an early start.

2. *From the main car park turn left for a short distance on the road towards Yealand
Redmayne, take the first gate on the right and enter through a kissing gate onto the path
which runs parallel with the road. A short pause by the seat on this path gives excellent
views across the reed bed with the possibility of distant flight views of marsh harrier and
bittern. After a short return to the road, take the right turn down the causeway across*

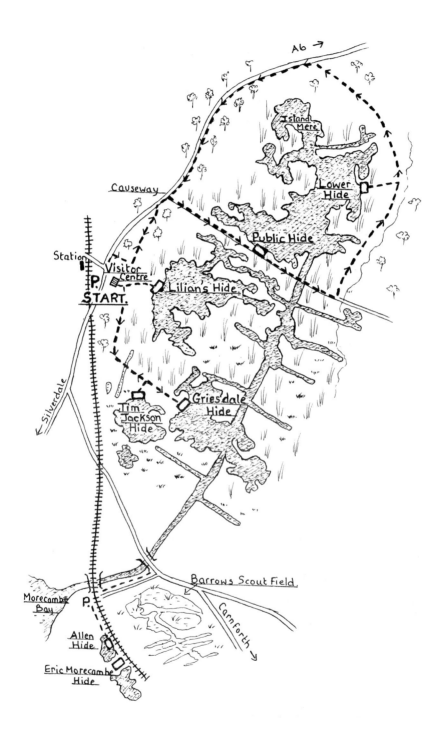

the centre of the reserve towards the public and lower hides. All the hides are signposted, with the distance to each.

The causeway with its willow screening often attracts flocks of tits, and in the spring and summer warblers, especially reed, sedge and willow warblers, along with blackcap and chiffchaff. It is the best place to look for bearded tits throughout the year with the gaps in the willows allowing one to scan the reeds. The most reliable time to see this spectacular little bird is from mid-September to early November. Choose a reasonably calm morning, preferably sunny. The first clue as to their presence is usually the distinctive 'pinging' call. At this time of year the newly moulted birds flock and from about 9.00 to 11.00 are at their most active. At times they collect grit to facilitate digestion and in the first gap on the right two grit trays have been provided at the perfect distance to give wonderful views of small groups actively gritting and interacting. Most of the birds are colour ringed as part of a population study.

Many visitors come to hear the extraordinary booming call of the bittern and the causeway is the best place to hear it from. The birds often start in February with a short tuning up period when the call is more a croak than a full throated boom, but gradually the power increases and they are in full voice by mid-March. From the causeway it is possible to be close enough to hear the intake of air into the specially modified oesophagus for the bird to produce the amazing foghorn sound which is used to proclaim the male's territory ownership and of course to attract the females.

Kestrel (photo by C. Dodding)

One feature you may notice as you walk down the causeway is the old stone gate posts. The most noticeable are by the causeway bridge and provide evidence of its former agricultural status as rich arable land. From 1840 to 1917, the Leighton valley was drained by a complex of dykes and a series of steam-driven pumps and was known as the 'Golden Valley' because of the abundant crops, roots and cereal it produced. However in 1917 during the First World War coal was scarce, the pumps were stopped and the area allowed to reflood. Since then nature has reclaimed the area and transformed it into a reed fen so we now have another 'Golden Valley'.

The causeway is also a good place to search for the secretive water rail. Their squealing call can be heard throughout the year, but achieving a sighting is usually more a question of luck except during frosty spells when the water by the causeway bridge remains unfrozen and can offer the right conditions to attract them out of the reeds.

The public hide overlooks the largest area of water on the reserve and is probably the best for diving ducks, with good views of pochard and tufted duck throughout the year and goldeneye and goosander in winter. Scan the surrounding limestone hills and woods for soaring buzzards and passing ravens, as both have increased markedly in recent years.

The path to the lower hide passes through the edge of the fen. This area is partly dominated by willows but also by the large tussocks of the aptly named Tussock Sedge. Unlike woodland, a fen is a riot of colour throughout the growing season with yellow flag iris, marsh valerian, ragged robin, and Devil's bit scabious just a few of the succession of flowers which grace this area. Breeding birds here include sedge warblers and reed buntings along with the occasional grasshopper warbler. In winter mixed flocks of siskin, redpoll and goldfinch feed in the fringeing alders.

The lower hide gives the best light condition during the morning. Reed warblers and reed buntings breed close to the hide. Wildfowl are similar to those seen from the public hide, although the shallow water areas close to the hide are well used by teal and shoveler, with gargeney in most springs. Bitterns can be looked for from all the reserve's hides but this hide is probably the best for this difficult species in winter. The dead trees at the back of the mere are well used by grey herons and cormorants and occasionally by passing ospreys. Scan the fields on the hillside for browsing roe and fallow deer.

3. *From the lower hide follow the path around the head of the valley and out onto the road. Turn left and eventually re-join the path just past the causeway entrance then either return to the visitor centre for a welcome coffee or follow the signs to Lilian's, Tim Jackson and Griesdale hides. If you made an early arrival call at the visitor centre to obtain your permit then consult the information display for news of the latest sightings.*

The path from the lower hides passes through willow woodland and then limestone woodland – both are excellent for the commoner woodland birds.

Lilian's hide gives excellent views over the mere and the extensive reedbeds and is usually the best hide to watch the breeding marsh harriers. Early in the spring they undertake spectacular 'sky diving' displays interspersed with bouts of nest building. As the season progresses the male is much in evidence as he brings food to the nesting females, and on occasions one polygamous male has provisioned three females. When the young are being fed the females cause havoc by making regular forays into the black-headed gull colony to take the young birds. The smaller males tend to hunt on the fields and marshes away from the reserve. Black-headed gulls often provide a clue to anything unusual for they regularly mob birds such as bitterns and herons as they fish along the reed edge. For much of the year this hide is the best place to witness the evening spectacular as thousands of starlings, swallows and sand martins come in to roost in the reedbeds. The spectacle is further heightened by the appearance of up to three sparrowhawks intent on catching a meal. At times peregrine and hobby also put in an appearance. Other roosting birds include smaller numbers of pied wagtail, and in the willows redwing and fieldfare.

The Tim Jackson and Griesdale hides are best for the surface feeding ducks, especially teal, shoveler, gadwall, wigeon and at times pintail. Summer evenings very often give the best viewing with good numbers of wildfowl and waders including large numbers of black-tailed godwit in recent years. Red deer regularly occur in numbers wading in the water and grazing the succulent iris and reed. From June onwards the hinds bring out their calves, which give an entertaining show as they race each other along the dry banks. In October several stags may be seen roaring at each other during the annual rut and if you are lucky you may witness a jousting match. From spring to early autumn as your return at dusk to the car park watch out for bats, of which five species occur, including the largest British bat, the noctule and the commonest, the pipistrelle.

4. *The route can be varied to suit both long and short walks. The best areas for bird watching depend also on the time of arrival and the season. The short walk is just to visit the three hides closest to the visitor centre, fine for a late afternoon or evening visit and these hides often give the best bird watching in winter. There is usually plenty to occupy a full day at Leighton but for more variety, especially during spring and autumn passage, this walk can be combined with a visit to the two hides overlooking the shore pools (walk no. 16) or some of the other walks in the Silverdale area.*

Jenny Brown's Point, the shore pools and Wood Well

Hawfinch.

Start: Starts and returns to the Allen and Eric
Morecambe RSPB car park
Grid reference: SD 476737
Distance: 7.5 km (4.7 miles)
Time: Allow 4 to 6 hours
Grade: Easy to moderate.
General: Toilets, tea room and shop at Leighton Moss
visitor centre and in Silverdale.

THIS WALK TAKES IN ONE OF THE BEST high tide roost and sea watching points at Jenny Brown's Point – the brackish lagoons on the salt marsh near Leighton Moss – and returns via the limestone woodland so typical of the Arnside/Silverdale Area. It is best to pick a midday spring tide (8.5–9.0m) and time yourself to arrive at Jenny Brown's Point at least an hour before high tide. Walks at low tide or on neap tides are not as productive, but the shore pools are always worth a visit. It is of course possible to do the walk in reverse to coincide with tidal conditions.

1. *Park in the RSPB car park at the end of the track, which runs alongside the Quicksand Pool Dyke. Take the path signposted to the Allen and Eric Morecambe hides.*

The rough grassland, reeds and scrub alongside the path often harbours many birds especially at passage periods. Reed bunting and sedge warbler are common breeders, with a least one pair of grasshopper warblers in recent years. During passage periods flocks of tits and warblers occur along with birds such as whinchat and stonechat, and both barn and short–eared owl have been recorded hunting over the open areas. In autumn and winter, flocks of redwing and fieldfare are attracted by the hawthorn berries.

The two hides give excellent views across the lagoons and the salt marsh. The second hide has the larger vista but the birds are similar so they are described together. The star breeding bird here is the avocet and increasing numbers have bred since one pair colonised in 2001. They are usually present from mid-March to early September, the shallow water providing plenty of scope for them to use their uniquely upturned bills to sieve out the shrimps and other invertebrates. Large numbers of noisy black-headed gulls breed on the many islands, and in recent years the handsome Mediterranean gull has bred on occasions. Other breeding birds include skylark, meadow pipit, lapwing, redshank, pochard, shoveler and gadwall.

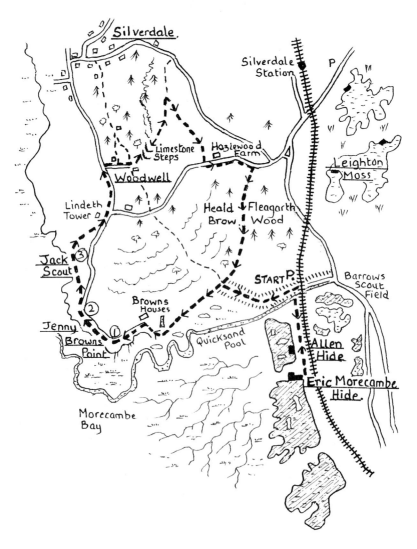

Jenny Browns Point

C. Dodding.

Given the right water conditions passage waders occur in numbers especially on autumn passage. The commonest are black-tailed godwit, redshank, lapwing, greenshank, dunlin, ruff, spotted redshank and green sandpiper. In a good year these are joined by curlew sandpiper and little stint and the pools have quite an impressive list of rarities, including pectoral sandpiper and black-winged pratincole. Peregrine and Merlin regularly hunt the pools, scattering the wader flocks and in spring and early summer the Leighton Moss marsh harriers regularly quarter the marsh.

From late summer onwards the numbers of wildfowl start to build up and by October large numbers of wigeon, shoveler, pintail, teal, gadwall and shelduck assemble. A regular flock of greylag geese grazes the salt marshes, joined at times by pinkfeet, Canada and barnacle geese. Wildfowl numbers peak in early winter and the brackish pools freeze later than fresh water, so numbers often build up at the start of a cold spell as birds are displaced from inland. Herons are regular throughout the year but peak numbers occur as the water levels start to drop in early summer and gatherings of up to 20 exploit the abundant fish. With them are annually increasing numbers of little egret.

Before setting out on the next leg of the walk it is well worth walking back a short distance along the access road under the railway bridge to view the reed bed re-creation area of Barrow Scout. At the time of writing the open water and grassland is good for both wildfowl and waders and stonechat occur throughout the year, although as the reed encroaches the species will no doubt change to be more like Leighton Moss.

2. *Return to the car park and take the footpath over the bridge and follow the path towards Jenny Brown's Point. Note that the footpath now runs along the top of the embankment and not across the fields as shown on OS maps.*

The walk on the embankment gives good views across the salt marsh and over the re-claimed fields of Quaker Stang. Geese and waders often use these fields especially when they are partially flooded.

3. *The path to Jenny Brown's Point passes along the edge of the salt marsh before turning onto the road past Jenny Brown's cottages. There are three good vantage points to watch from at the Point: (1) from the seat overlooking the salt marsh (2) the walled area with a stile a little further on (3) the so-called Bride's Seat on the highest point within the Nation Trust Jack Scout area. Telescopes are essential at all three sites.*

Wood Well – a haunt of amphibians as well as woodland birds including the elusive hawfinch. Today's visitors will notice several changes.
(photo taken c.1961 by D. Hindle)

The first site overlooks the salt marsh where vast flocks of oystercatcher, curlew and smaller numbers of knot, dunlin, redshank, bar-tailed godwit, shelduck, red-breasted merganser, cormorant and pintail assemble at high tide. Turnstones and the occasional purple sandpiper frequent the rocky breakwater. The other two sites are best for watching the wader roost assemble and for sea watching. The choice of site depends on the weather, the wall giving some shelter from westerly winds – the best conditions for sea watching – and you need patience for this type of birding, as you need to be continually scanning the sea for fleeting sightings. However, a dedicated small group of observers spends hours there, so you may well have company. Given the right conditions and season, numbers of gannets, kittiwakes, fulmars, eider, red-throated diver and Arctic terns occur. The site is rapidly becoming established as a migration watch point for the passage of pomarine, great and Arctic skuas, Manx shearwater, Leach's and storm petrel.

4. *After passing through the National Trust area, return to the road and continue towards Silverdale. Turn right off the road and down the track where it is signposted Wood Well, opposite the plant nursery.*

This is an excellent area for woodland birds so look out for marsh tit, nuthatch, treecreeper, green and great spotted woodpeckers, and in spring blackcap and garden warbler. This is a well known site for the elusive hawfinch; always difficult, but the best plan is to scan the tops of the trees as soon as you turn down the track, for they often perch in this exposed position. A short diversion into the wood on the left just before the well can be productive, as can searching the trees on either side of the field that almost runs up to the well. Listen for its call, the 'ticking of an angry robin'. A calm early morning in late winter and spring gives the best chance of spotting this elusive species.

5. *From the Well take the path that goes up the limestone crag, bear left and then right again on leaving the wood. At the road turn left and pass Hazelwood Farm and the entrance to Hazelwood nursing home. Continue until the first path on the right which takes you through Fleagarth Wood and eventually re-join the outward path onto the embankment at the foot of Heald Brow.*

Fleagarth is another good woodland site. Besides the birds mentioned under Wood Well check out the yews for breeding goldcrest and in autumn for vast flocks of redwing and fieldfare, which feast on this bounteous harvest for a few weeks.

Haweswater Gait Barrows and Silverdale Moss

Reed Warbler   C.D.

Start: Starts and ends at Silverdale railway station
Grid reference: SD475751
Distance: 8 km (5 miles)
Time: Allow 5 to 6 hours
Grade: Easy
General: Toilets, tea room and shop at Leighton Moss
visitor centre or Waterslack garden centre

THIS WALK THROUGH THE VARIED HABITATS and scenery around Silverdale can either be started at Silverdale railway station or from the small informal roadside car park near Challan Hall. It traverses the limestone pavement of Gait Barrows National Nature Reserve, and leaflets describing the trails there can be downloaded from www.english-nature.org. It also skirts the large RSPB reed bed restoration project on Silverdale Moss.

1. *Turn right out of the railway station and continue along the road past the small hamlet of houses and Moss Lane, and take the footpath on the right which takes you across the railway then along the edge of Haweswater Moss via the permissive path until it joins the main path to Haweswater. Those parking at the roadside will follow the main track to Haweswater and pick up the route here.*

In spring listen for the boom of the Leighton Moss bitterns because as soon as you leave the train you can usually hear them above the raucous calls of black-headed gulls. The first part of the route usually produces very little except flocks of fieldfares and redwing in early winter which feed on any apples left in the large orchard to the left. Once off the road the view over Haweswater moss and lake is excellent and marsh harriers are now regular summer visitors to this small reed bed, as are sedge and reed warblers, while

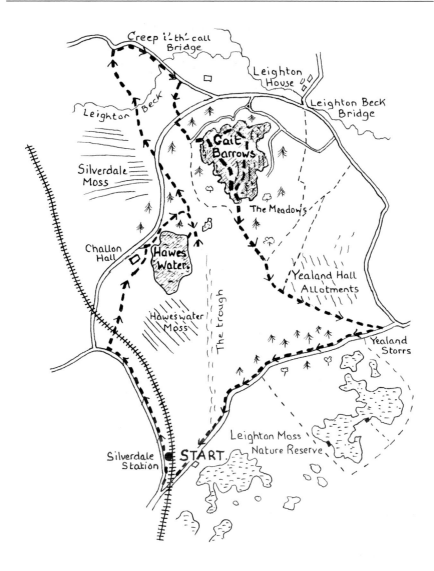

water rails and reed buntings are resident. The succession of flowers over the fence along the Moss edge is well worth examination, with yellow flag iris in June, through marsh valerian, ragged robin in midsummer and hemp agrimony in late summer.

2. *Follow the main track taking the first path right through a gated meadow and then down the stub path to Haweswater edge. Retracing your steps for a short distance, follow the path right which leads to the boardwalk along the edge of Haweswater, then complete this short circuit by returning to the start of the stub track to Haweswater and continue along the edge of the meadow and through the woodland, heading for Silverdale Moss.*

The woods here are good for marsh tits, quite a common resident throughout the Silverdale area. Both green and greater spotted woodpeckers occur, as do nuthatch. The meadow is excellent for butterflies, many attracted by the hemp agrimony and knapweed, then in late summer look out for high brown fritillary and wall brown. The meadow is also good for dragon and damsel flies and for the brown hawker, our largest dragonfly, in late summer.

There are several good views over Haweswater but as the largest natural lake in Lancashire it is very deep, so numbers of wildfowl are low, usually a few goldeneye and tufted duck in winter. However during frosty spells when the lake because of its depth is ice free, numbers of teal and shoveler are displaced from Leighton. Ospreys occasionally use the dead trees for perching and sparrowhawk, buzzard, peregrine and raven regularly fly overheads.

The edge of Haweswater has exceptional botanical interest, with bird's eye primrose in spring, such delights as pyramidal and fragrant orchids and dark red helleborine in summer, and lots of other specialities throughout the growing season.

3. *Follow the path around the outside of the meadow then away through the woods to cross the road and down towards Silverdale Moss. The path skirts the edge of Silverdale Moss and passes over Leighton Beck and eventually comes out on the road.*

The woodlands in this part of the walk are good for breeding chiffchaff and blackcap, with a few garden warblers in the scrubbier parts of the area. Goldcrests also breed, often linked with areas of yew.

Silverdale Moss is the main RSPB site for reed bed restoration in the area. An area of former poor grazing land is carefully being turned into a reed bed by planting and raising the water table. As the reed becomes established, hopefully many of the Leighton Moss specialities will spread there. At the time of writing it has already attracted hunting marsh harriers and breeding lapwing, shoveler, gadwall and curlew. In winter large flocks of wigeon, pintail, shoveler and lapwing are regular. Views from the footpath are rather distant but it is worth lingering a while as the spectacle is most impressive, particularly when the wildfowl are flushed by a visiting peregrine or buzzard.

4. *When reaching the road turn right and over Leighton Beck Bridge (or as it is marked on some maps 'Creep i'-th'-call Bridge') until the small reserve of the Landscape Trust, Coldwell Parrock, is reached. Cross this on the permissive path, turn right onto the road for a short distance before entering Gait Barrows National Nature Reserve.*

Woodland birds predominate but Coldwell Parrock is excellent for breeding garden warblers. A wonderful sight among the many cowslips or early purple orchids of spring is a visiting green woodpecker searching for ants.

5. *Once in Gait Barrows, follow the track until the large display board by the second gate. Here one has a choice of routes which are clearly shown on the map and the display board and are well way-marked. The yew trail – marked purple on the map is the longest and keeps mainly to the wooded areas, while the white marked limestone trail passes over the limestone pavement. In both cases they eventually lead into the meadow to rejoin the public footpath. Alternatively, if time is short you can just follow the public footpath through the reserve.*

Gait Barrows has so much to offer the naturalist and geologist. The remarkable limestone pavement has the most diverse flora in Britain, ranging from the bonsai ash and yew trees growing within the grykes, to such national rarities as angular Solomon's seal, pale St John's wort, rigid buckler fern, limestone fern and dark red helleborine. Butterflies abound, with the Duke of Burgundy fritillary which thrives in the sheltered glades flying in June and where the caterpillars feed on the abundant cowslips. Much of the woodland is carefully coppiced to provide ideal conditions for violets. They are the food plants of the caterpillars of three other declining fritillaries, high brown, pearl-bordered and small pearl-bordered. Not to be overlooked are the wood ants – over 30,000 can be found in one nest or mound. They 'farm' aphids and search for insect prey in the woodlands.

The birds are very typical of the Silverdale/Arnside limestone woodlands. The yew walk probably gives the best selection throughout the year, with a good range of warblers, including blackcap, chiffchaff and garden warbler. This area though really comes into its own from mid-October and on into November when the yews produce an abundance of fruit, attracting large mixed flocks of redwing, fieldfare, blackbird and mistle thrush. Marsh tits regularly take the fruit, as do greenfinch, and in some years a small flock of hawfinch is attracted by the colourful berries.

6. *From the point where the track reaches the meadow, follow the well marked path across the meadow and into the scrub and woodland known as Yealand Hall allotments.*

The scrub is good for breeding warblers including willow and garden warblers, blackcap, and lesser whitethroat. In autumn the large thrush flocks, described for Gait Barrows, also visit the many yew trees. Buzzards and ravens are regular.

7. *On reaching the road turn right down the hill, continue past Leighton Moss and return to Silverdale railway station or, if parked near Haweswater, follow the first set of instructions.*

This final stretch can be quite productive giving good views over Leighton Moss, with the chance of hunting marsh harriers or even an osprey perched on the dead trees. Two of the meres are visible from the road so a good selection of wildfowl may be added to the day's list. The fields on the other side of the road to the first mere are good for little owls and, in late winter, flocks of redwing and fieldfare are regular, with a grazing flock of feral greylag and Canada geese. In spring at dawn and dusk woodcock undertake their 'roding' flights, often flying right above the road. The woodlands are also good for the common woodland birds, giving a last chance to pick up birds such as treecreeper, marsh tit, long-tailed tit and goldcrest.

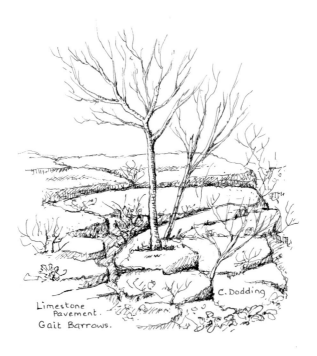

Limestone
Pavement.
Gait Barrows.

C. Dodding

The two Arnsides:
a coastal circular via Far Arnside

Green
Woodpecker   C.D.

Start:	This circular walk starts and finishes at Arnside railway station
Grid reference:	461788
Distance:	9 km (5.6 miles)
Time:	Allow 5 hours
Grade:	Easy to moderate
General:	Refreshment, toilet and car parking facilities at Arnside
	♿ Wheelchair access at Arnside promenade to view the Kent estuary and at Arnside Knott car park to view the woodlands and Morecambe Bay

THE SMALL COASTAL SETTLEMENT OF ARNSIDE is thought to take its name from a Viking called Arnulf when it became his family saetr or seat. Before the coming of the railway Arnside, Sandside and Milnthorpe flourished as small estuarine ports. The railway first came to Arnside in 1857 and further established the Victorian resort with its characteristic Victorian opulent shops and houses. A major feature of the landscape emerged when the Ulverston and Lancaster Railway Co. built the 550 metre-long Kent viaduct, designed by James Brunskill, thus completing this section of the railway before it was absorbed by the Furness Railway in 1862. Almost a century later and armed with the *Observer's* book of birds, the author frantically identified his first oystercatcher, heron, curlew and redshank from a Millom-bound train in the late 1950s! While the Kent viaduct substantially changed the topography of

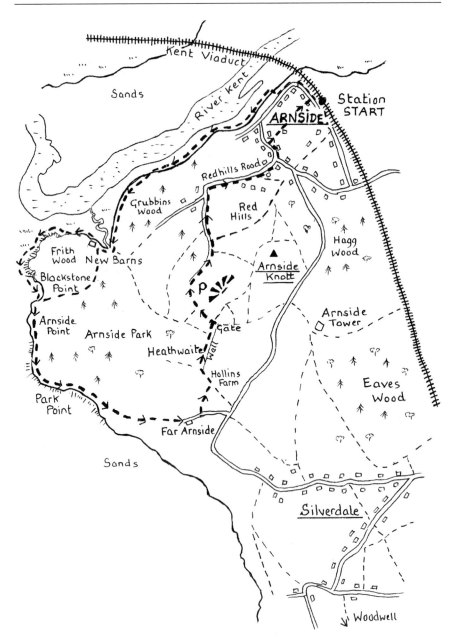

the estuary, today little has changed and trains still trundle over its girders, but thank goodness for good field guides and optics!

It is recommended to commence the walk about one and a half hours before high water, when bird activity is more pronounced, preferably coinciding with the tidal spectacle of the 'Kent bore'. At Arnside a siren warns of the incoming tide. After witnessing the initial tidal surge or bore, which varies enormously in strength and speed, you will be amazed how quickly the tide submerges the bay's inter-tidal sand flats. **Keep off the inter-tidal areas**.

1. *From the station turn right onto the road to reach the promenade overlooking the Kent Estuary and continue straight past the Albion public house onto a concrete footpath indicated as 'New Barns.' After passing the coastguard station, the path ends on the pebble beach before regaining a track leading past cottages at New Barns bay and onto Blackstone Point and White Creek woodland caravan site. At the caravan site follow a footpath sign to Far Arnside, via the scenic cliff top footpath and the limestone promontory of Park Point. Be aware that between White Creek and Far Arnside the footpath follows the edge of low limestone cliffs that are potentially dangerous. At certain stages of the highest tides an alternative route may be sought leading from the terraced cottages at New Barn to Far Arnside.*

2. *Enter Arnside Park woodland and follow the footpath through Holgate's caravan site emerging at the hamlet of Far Arnside. Proceed along a minor lane to Hollin's Farm and there follow a footpath left along the edge of a field with a wall on the right to reach Heathwaite. At a cross roads follow the footpath signs to Arnside, via the summit of Arnside Knott while enjoying superb views, including the vista of Lake District mountains identifiable with the well placed toposcope. From the car park descend the lower slopes of the Knott along a tarmac road that joins Redhills Road. Turn right into Redhills Road and continue for nearly a kilometre to the junction with Silverdale Road. Turn left into Silverdale Road and first right into Chapel Lane. Proceed along a narrow footpath that eventually descends to the railway station.*

3. *On reaching Far Arnside there is also a choice to walk to Silverdale railway station via Eaves Wood or alternatively via the coastal route and Woodwell. If doing either walk to Silverdale then consult the appropriate Ordnance Survey Maps.*

The sandflats and channel of the River Kent adjacent to Arnside Marsh, viewable from the south platform of Arnside Station, often has flocks of redshank, oystercatcher, lapwing and curlew, while ringed plover and golden plover are less common. In autumn occasional little stint, curlew sandpiper and greenshank occur. Scrutinising the waders may pay dividends, for rare American vagrant waders have occurred here. Take a close look at gulls for amongst five or six regular species there is a possibility of seeing the yellow-legged gull, an uncommon visitor from Mediterranean climes, which has been recorded either side of the railway viaduct.

Arnside promenade provides an opportunity to observe the main channel before its emergence into the bay. Take a walk down the pier west of the railway viaduct, built by the railway company in order to compensate for the loss of trade further up river when ships could no longer reach Milnthorpe. Here time has stood still, with typical flocks of mallard, redshank, lapwing, oystercatcher, curlew, and sentinel like heron and cormorant. At the west end of the promenade, winter flocks of chaffinches mixed with brambling have been recorded feeding on the beech mast in the grounds of Ashmeadow. Close by a low cliff is a small clump of the rare but beautiful maiden hair fern. At New Barns the calls of alarmed redshank may herald your presence but take a look at the smaller birds rising from the small marsh that may include skylark, meadow pipit, pied and grey wagtail and, in spring and autumn, the conspicuous markings of the handsome wheatear.

The cliff top footpath between White Creek and Arnside Point affords an opportunity to bird-watch the bay and perhaps even to indulge in luncheon! One exceptional sighting here was of a pod of pilot whales. Birds can be a bit thin on the ground in summer but passage highlights have included skuas, red-throated diver, short-eared owl and storm-driven sea birds. Winter wildfowl and wader flocks feature wigeon, teal, mallard, shelduck, goosander, great crested grebe, red-breasted merganser, ringed plover, lapwing, curlew, knot, oystercatcher dunlin and redshank. Do not be surprised, however, if an otherwise peaceful scene is suddenly interrupted by a peregrine falcon or a merlin, causing panic as it dives into a flock of waders before flying off with a preferred tasty morsel.

In complete contrast, bird tables at Far Arnside caravan park attract nuthatch, marsh tit, bullfinch, greenfinch, dunnock, great spotted woodpecker, blackbird and song thrush and in turn this live bait may just occasionally prove irresistible to a patrolling sparrowhawk. Here also rather curious and quite tame roe deer come out of the woodlands to encroach into the residents' neat little gardens. Take a close look at the garden furniture for that cute, plastic facsimile 'Bambi' might just be the real thing, shamelessly creating mayhem and without green fingers!

Heathwaite and Arnside Knott with its wooded slopes and limestone screes is a botanically rich area, protected by the National Trust. It is today the haunt of raven, jackdaw, jay, kestrel, buzzard, mistle thrush, warblers, goldcrest, treecreeper, nuthatch, green and great spotted woodpecker. Of the summer visitors to the broad-leafed woodlands the willow warbler is probably the commonest, while lesser whitethroats may occasionally be located in the tangles of undergrowth by its intermittent yet distinctive song. Other harbingers of spring include chiffchaff, blackcap and garden warbler, but nowadays redstarts and tree pipit do not seem to favour this apparently suitable habitat. Resident treecreepers may be watched in any suitable wooded locality, including gardens, steadfastly picking their way up a tree trunk searching every crevice for insects before a repeat performance on the next tree.

Arnside Knott's weather beaten juniper scrub and gnarled yew trees have withstood the passage of time over hundreds of years and the berries have sustained winter thrushes of Scandinavian origin such as redwing and fieldfare. To be honest, the birding potential is good but not *that* good. Arnside Knott is renowned for its mixture of southern and northern species diversity at the edge of their range with profusions of traveller's joy or old man's beard, deadly nightshade that most certainly lives up to its name, and the extremely localised spiked speedwell. In the woods there are colonies of the southern wood ant, while the slopes rising to the summit of the Knott are endowed with blue moor grass that is the food plant of an isolated but thriving colony of the Scotch argus butterfly. Other rare butterflies are present on the Knott but amongst the commoner gems to be encountered are brimstone, wall brown, speckled wood, red admiral, peacock, comma, painted lady, large, small and green-veined white, meadow brown, orange tip and small tortoiseshell. In summer the common lizard may be seen on the paths and limestone where it is quite at home enjoying a spot of sunbathing! Mammals include roe deer, brown hare, rabbit, stoat and weasel. It is, however, unfortunate that the native red squirrel is probably extinct having been superseded by the invasive and ubiquitous grey squirrel throughout the AONB.

Walking back though Arnside along an interesting narrow footpath linking Chapel Lane to the railway station now provides a focus for garden birds, which include nuthatch, great spotted woodpecker, song thrush, blackbird, chaffinch, titmice, dunnock, greenfinch and robin. Listen for the chirpings of house sparrows for nowadays sightings of this increasingly officially endangered species are worth recording. Do not be fooled by the murmurings of starlings for the bird is an excellent mimic. Nowadays that Asiatic invader of the 1960s, the collared dove, is well established at Arnside and seems to call incessantly. Flocks of jackdaws are predominant in the urban setting and nest in local quarries and sometimes chimney pots! But wildlife aside the two Arnsides are well worth exploring if only for the superb views of Morecambe Bay and Lakeland's mountains at various points of the walk.

Kent Viaduct from Arnside Knott.

C. Dodding

Walking the river Kent at Kendal

Lesser black-backed gull

Start: Start at Helsington Mill (SD513905) and finish at Sandy Bottoms at the confluence of the rivers Kent and Mint

Grid reference: SD517944

Distance: 5.5 km (3.4 miles)

Time: Allow 3 to 4 hours

Grade: Easy riverside walk through Kendal

General: Refreshment and toilet facilities are available in Kendal at Abbot Hall, Miller Bridge and other easily accessible establishments. Limited car parking facilities at Helsington Mill Sections of this walk in Kendal town centre are suitable for wheelchair access to view the river

THIS PLEASANT RIVERSIDE WALK is particularly suitable for bird watchers and historians. It explores the upper reaches of the River Kent from pastoral farmland south of Kendal, through the urban landscape of the historic town, to re-emerge north into countryside at Sandy Bottoms by the rivers Kent and Mint confluence. The River Mint may even remind you to fortify yourself with a slab of the famous Kendal Mint Cake as well as a small flask of coffee. A good time for this walk is early on a pristine Sunday morning in late winter or early spring when the town is quiet and you can take in the birds, scenery and Kendal's historic buildings and bridges. You might be gone for some time but there is just a chance that you might make Sunday lunch! Although we strongly recommend the full walk, the beauty of

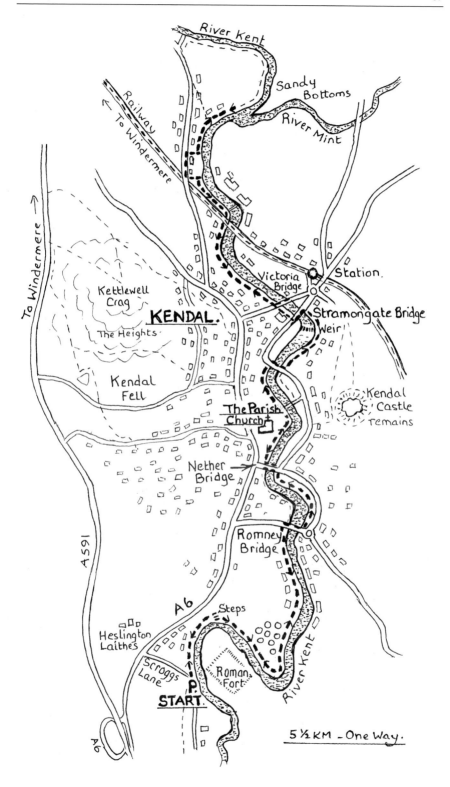

Walking the river Kent at Kendal

River Kent

Sandy Bottoms

River Mint

Railway
← To Windermere

To Windermere →

Kettlewell Crag

KENDAL.

The Heights

Kendal Fell

Victoria Bridge

Station.

Stramongate Bridge

Weir

Kendal Castle remains

The Parish Church

Nether Bridge

A591

Romney Bridge

Steps

Heslington Laithes

A6

Scroggs Lane

Roman Fort

P.
START.

A6

River Kent

5½ KM - One Way.

this walk is that it can be commenced or left at any point in the town and is easily reached from Kendal railway station.

On a normal walk expect to see around forty species in both the rural and urban environments of Kendal. The emphasis is on the waterbirds with anything else being a bonus. Rarities are exceptional although in the past this has been countered by sightings of ring-necked duck and night heron. From the time of the millennium thirty five surveys have been undertaken over a five-year period and sixty seven species have been recorded by Kendal birder, Gordon Clarke. We acknowledge his help in supplying the data which is required for ongoing wetland conservation research by the Wetland Bird Survey.

Close to the starting point of this walk, the Tudor manor house of Helsington Laithes has adorned the landscape of the old county of Westmorland since the late 15th century. Local government reform in 1969 led to the absorption of Westmorland, Cumberland and parts of Lancashire into the county of Cumbria. Kendal was the former administrative centre of Westmorland and apart from the town's newspaper the *Westmorland Gazette* perpetuating the name of the old county it has now been consigned to oblivion.

1. *The starting point to the walk may be reached by car or Stagecoach bus 555 from the A591 via the A6 to Kendal south. If approaching from the south, turn right at the roundabout and after approximately 300 yards turn eastwards off the A6 along Scroggs Lane to Helsington Mill. Commence the walk by taking the path on the west bank of the River Kent north towards Kendal, emerging from woodland to turn right down some steps before reaching the sewage farm on the left. Follow the path along the river and after reaching Romney Bridge turn right over the bridge and left to reach K Village, as the former shoe factory is now known. Keep left on the riverside footpath to reach Nether Bridge. Cross over to regain the west bank, immediately cutting through to reach the riverside walk which leads past the parish church at Miller Bridge. Do not cross but continue to New Road, where, should you need it, there is a toilet on the car park.*

2. *At the north end of New Road turn right over a footbridge to Goose Holme. Follow the footpath to the weir and Stramongate Bridge. Crossing the bridge continue north along the west bank passing Victoria Bridge and Sandes Avenue to reach the Magistrate's Court. Here the path divides so take the right fork following the river under the Windermere railway line. After surveying the river from an old footbridge, stay on the west bank and pass through an iron gate, temporarily leaving the river behind. At the first opportunity turn right through a ginnel to reach the river and turn left along a cul-de-sac to Burneside Road. Turn right passing Aikrigg House on the right, and immediately right again between two houses to the river. Turn left along the riverside path to Sandy Bottoms to conclude the walk. Consider the possible use of the local bus service (no regular Sunday service) or taxi to return to the starting point. Alternatively, enjoy the walk back to Helsington which takes at least an hour.*

The riverside path first of all bisects Woodland Trust woodland, with the River Kent on the right, and passes house gardens on the left. Commence bird watching immediately by carefully observing the woodland, river banks, open water and weir. In the tangles of shrub and woodland cover look out for wren, robin, dunnock and in spring, blackcap, chiffchaff and willow warbler.

Throughout this walk characteristic birds associated with rivers, including dipper and kingfisher, and waders such as oystercatcher and wintering redshank, may be observed. Resident flocks of goosander are now commonly found almost anywhere along the River Kent. During April and May, in order of arrival, expect to see sand martin, swallow, common sandpiper, house martin and swift.

The weirs are a favoured locality for grey and pied wagtail as well as the dipper, whose vocalisations in early spring and semi-aquatic behaviour combine for a virtuoso performance that is well worth observing. The resident, long-staying domestic geese are nothing to get excited about but on this river the occasional pochard and tufted duck are more significant. Flocks of mallard are resident and in winter small numbers of goldeneye are encountered together with moorhen, coot and a little grebe lurking in the still waters. In autumn listen for the dulcet and evocative calls of flocks of pink-footed geese migrating from Iceland to wintering grounds on the Ribble at Martin Mere, while flocks of greylag geese of dubious origin engender less appeal.

The woodlands, gardens and open areas regularly support resident great spotted woodpecker, wood pigeon, collared dove, song thrush, mistle thrush, nuthatch, long tailed tit, coal tit, blue tit, great tit, goldcrest, treecreeper, jackdaw, chaffinch, greenfinch, bullfinch, goldfinch and the occasional marsh tit. The gardens regularly attract many of the usual suspects and in late winter are often joined by siskin and brambling. In autumn redwing and fieldfares feed on berry-laden hedgerows around Kendal and sometimes come into gardens during severe winter conditions.

Sparrowhawks can be expected almost anywhere hunting for small birds in the vicinity of gardens. Other raptors likely to be seen include the resident kestrel and buzzard, while peregrine falcons visit the area on hunting forays from more suitable terrain further north. Ravens have expanded south from the Lake District and need to be distinguished from the commoner carrion crow and rook, while the ever-present jackdaw present less of an identification problem.

Opposite the woodland on the east side of the river is the site of Watercrook Roman fort (Alvana). The sewage farm appears on the left, but no need to hold your breath for this modernised site holds far fewer birds than it used to in the good old days when primitive sewage farms were major havens for all sort of rarities – a downside to hygienic living! Take a moment of reflection and look back along the river, where wildfowl and little grebe may be visible under the steep riverbank and if you are very lucky you might even see some leaping salmon to add to the diversity on offer.

Moving off, kingfishers may sometimes be observed as a flash of blue or perched in the willows. At the Romney Bridge and shoe factory site a heron may stand motionless like a sentinel patiently waiting for a meal and very often a dipper too. Onto one of Kendal's most historic bridges, the 14th-century Nether Bridge. The underside will reveal that it has been widened twice in the succeeding centuries. The ancient bridge complements Kendal's medieval heritage. The Parish Church of Holy Trinity has occupied its present site since 1232 and is considered to be the second widest five-aisled church in England after St Helens at Abingdon, Oxford.

The vicinity of Stramongate is a favoured site for the local black-headed gull and mallard population that never miss an opportunity for free handouts. All contributions are greedily received so why change the habit of a lifetime! Scrutinise the gulls for common gull, lesser black-backed and herring gull and consider the possibility of other less common species such as the Mediterranean gull, an increasing visitor to the area. Sharing the urban environment in Kendal there might be a few starlings or even a mind boggling house sparrow or two – such is the course of so called progress that both of these formerly familiar birds have now become of conservation concern and are now officially listed as red data species.

Another 14th-century bridge at Stramongate has survived along with the more youthful Victoria Bridge, built in 1887. Upon leaving the town traffic behind and enjoying the idyllic scene that becomes increasingly rural once more, there is a reminder of yet another Victorian enterprise in the form of the Windermere branch line which dates back to 1847, the heyday of railway construction.

On reaching Sandy Bottoms at the confluence of the rivers Kent and Mint, sit a while to get your breath back, take in the scene as well as a little refreshment and let the bird life come to you. Something usually does because the confluence of the two rivers is home to little grebe, dipper, grey wagtails, oystercatcher and goosander, and in winter tufted duck and goldeneye. Kingfisher will not be far away, and the surrounding trees often hold tits, warblers and finches.

Whitbarrow

silver wash fritillary

Start: Start at the small informal car park near
Witherslack Hall school
Grid reference: SD438861
Distance: 6 Km (3.7 miles)
Time: Allow 3 to 4 hours
Grade: Easy to moderate
General: Toilets refreshments and shops at
Grange-over-Sands

THIS WALK TRAVERSES THE LARGEST limestone hill around Morecambe Bay and also takes in the oak/ash woodland on its flanks. The views from the summit are superb both across the bay to the south and the Lakeland Fells to the north. Whitbarrow is at its best in spring and summer and this walk has much to delight the all-round naturalist. A leaflet and map of Whitbarrow can be downloaded from www.limestone-pavements.org.uk.

1. *Park in the small informal car park by the outbuildings of Witherslack Hall school and follow the path through the field and towards the permissive path through Witherslack woods.*

From the field gate there is an excellent view of the crag where peregrines and ravens breed. It is well worth pausing to scan the whole crag and continue to keep a watch on the crag as you walk across the field. These two cliff-nesting species regularly engage in pitched battles with the peregrine usually coming off best – a wonderful sight if you are lucky enough to be viewing the crag at the right time. Buzzards are also regular along the crag and over the wood and on occasions the peregrine will also engage with this larger species.

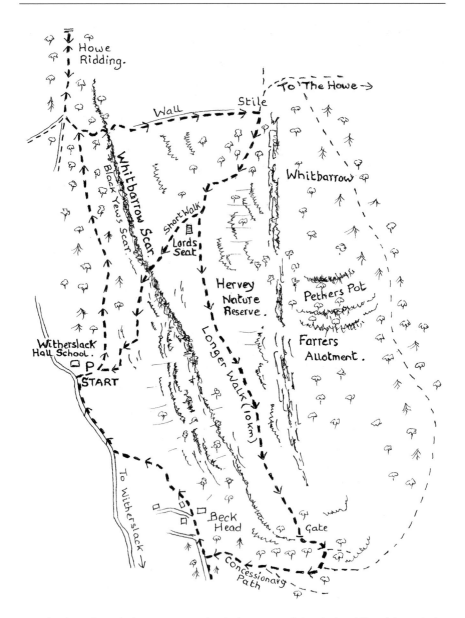

2. *Take the well marked permissive path which runs parallel with the cliff and through the oak/ ash woodlands of Witherslack woods.*

The first section passes close to a football field, where the scrubby woodland edge is good for willow and garden warblers. The more mature woodland has a healthy population of chiffchaff, blackcap, and garden warbler. The 'yaffle' call of the green woodpecker is regularly heard, suggesting a good population but they can be hard to locate in the dense woodland. The drumming of the great spotted woodpecker is easier to follow and good views are often available. Other common residents include bullfinch and marsh and long-tailed tits. Sparrowhawks are regular along with buzzards, which usually object to your presence with their mewing call. In autumn the yew trees and other berry-bearing shrubs provide food for flocks of redwing and fieldfare.

Many of the small passerines nest in the thick bramble under storey which has been encouraged in many areas by coppicing of the hazel. When in flower the bramble provides excellent nectaring for the special butterflies of the area – the rare high brown fritillary and the exquisitely named silver washed fritillary. Both are very active fliers and difficult to tell apart until they land when you can view the under wing. Both are on the wing in July and August. The recently coppiced areas are usually the best, especially where a shaft of sunlight catches the bramble. Of course butterflies are very weather dependent and usually only fly when the temperature is above 13°C and sunny and at least 17°C when cloudy. The commonest butterfly in this section is the speckled wood. This species prefers glades and shady situations and successive broods are on the wing from April to September.

3. *Watch out for the signposted right turn which leads up the escarpment and onto the top of the hill. However, before taking this path, continue along a stub path which takes you into the nature reserve of Howe Ridding wood. This track eventually comes to a dead end and here retrace your steps to the junction and on up the escarpment.*

This section of the wood is managed especially for butterflies and in consequence is the best area for several species. If you failed to find the rarer fritillaries in the first part of the wood this area offers the best chance, for besides the bramble there are stands of thistle and knapweed, both very attractive to butterflies. Depending on the season several other species are abundant here including meadow brown, common blue, comma, wall and a further fritillary identification puzzle, the dark green, another species that you need to see the under wing for conclusive identification. Birds occurring in this section are very similar to the areas already covered, although the coppice areas attract many warblers and tits and because of the open nature of the habitat are easier to find. Green woodpeckers are also easier here for they prefer the more open areas for ground feeding on the abundant ants.

4. *Retrace your steps back to the signposted and rather steep route up the escarpment and out of the woods onto the open limestone grassland area.*

The woodland edge is often the best area for several species. Here redstart and tree pipit occur along with many other woodland species already mentioned. Ravens and buzzards are regular, often seen to follow the narrow transition zone between woodland and grassland.

This is also a wonderful area for butterflies with good numbers of pearl and small pearl-bordered fritillaries in season. In July it is possible to see four species of fritillaries on the wing at once, small pearl-bordered, dark green, high brown and silver washed. Remember the caterpillars of the five fritillaries all feed on violets which are abundant both in the woodlands and grasslands. The other fritillary on the list –the Duke of Burgundy – belongs to another family – the metal marks. Its food plants are cowslip and primrose and this attractive but rare butterfly is on the wing in May and June. Take care to look for mammal tracks in any damp patches. Whitbarrow has a large badger population and both red and roe deer occur.

5. *Once in the grassland area there is a network of paths to choose from. The short route takes the path across the grassland to the east side then follows the path south and then southwest past Lord's Seat, a memorial to Canon Hervey, the founder of the Cumbria Wildlife Trust, and down the escarpment path to return to the car park near Witherslack Hall. The longer route follows the path along the eastern boundary of the grassland down to Farrer's Allotment. This passes through the area which is being converted back to grassland after many years under a blanket of Corsican pine. The path eventually loops back to the track down the escarpment.*

The birds, plants and butterflies are similar throughout but obviously, the longer one spends, the more one will see. The grassland is dominated by blue moor grass and a visit in spring, when it is in flower, will show the origin of its name. Many typical limestone plants are abundant such as birds-foot trefoil, rock rose, harebell and wild thyme. Scarcer plants include dark red helleborine, bee and fly orchid, carline thistle and dropwort.

Breeding birds on the grassland include wheatear, skylark and meadow pipit and a recent colonist is the stonechat. Yellowhammers were once a common breeding bird, but now only a few remain where there are scattered shrubs. Green woodpeckers regularly forage in the short grass areas and kestrels hover overhead, while peregrines, ravens and especially buzzards patrol the area.

Sunny days produce the greatest numbers of butterflies. Besides those already mentioned, small heath, grayling, green hairstreak peacock, small tortoiseshell and small copper are abundant. In some years the migrant painted lady and red admiral occur in large numbers.

Great spotted woodpecker

Flookborough, Sandgate and West Plain Marsh

Sheldduck — N.B.

Start: Starts and finishes at Cark & Cartmel railway station
Grid reference: SD 365762
Distance: 8 km (5 miles)
Time: Allow 4 to 5 hours
Grade: Easy
General: Toilets, refreshments and shops in Grange-over-Sands

THIS WALK TAKES IN ONE OF THE LARGER wader roosts on Morecambe Bay and is best undertaken between mid-September and mid-March. To enjoy this spectacle it is essential to get the right height of tide and to plan to arrive on the coastal path at the back of West Plain Marsh at least 30 minutes before high tide. The tide should be at least 9.5 metres (Liverpool height). Remember also that the tide is around 15 minutes behind the predicted Liverpool or Morecambe time. This rather restricts the suitable days but it is well worth planning to do the walk on such days for on lower tides the main wader roost is on the sand flats well out from the salt marsh. If doing the walk on a lower tide it is probably best to concentrate on the Sandgate Marsh area watching the wildfowl and waders assemble. The route follows the Cumbria Coastal Way for much of the time.

1. *The walk starts at Cark station. Turn right out of the station and pick up the signposted Cumbria Coastal Way for a short distance on the road before turning left onto a footpath*

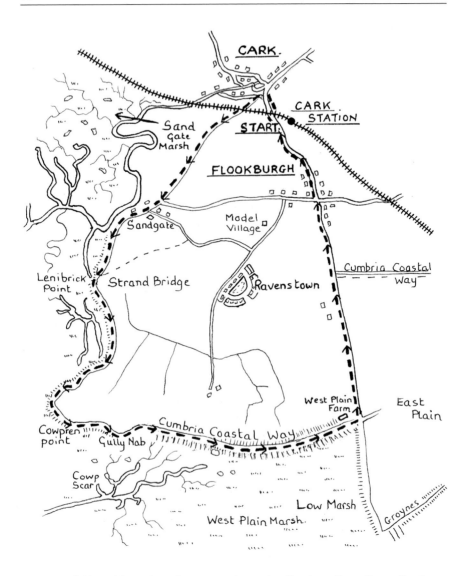

across fields and for a short distance on the road at Sandgate Farm. If travelling by car it is recommended to park in the signed car park in the centre of Flookborough village. Proceed down the main street towards Sand Gate Farm to pick up the Cumbria Coastal Way.

This first section features mainly farmland birds, including flocks of lapwing, fieldfare and redwing, the latter especially later in the winter when the berries are exhausted.

2. *From Sand Gate Farm follow the path out onto the edge of the salt marsh. From here the path hugs the edge of the marsh, following each indentation where the marsh joins* *the farmland. The path goes right to Cowpren Point where it picks up the old sea wall embankment.*

This section gives many good viewpoints over Sand Gate salt marsh and as the tide flows the movement of waders towards West Plain can be very impressive. These include large flocks of oystercatchers, curlew and redshank, many coming from the direction of Chapel Island. On lower tides they roost on exposed salt marsh but on the higher tides they head for West Plain Marsh. Wildfowl will sit out the tide, especially on calm days, and large numbers of wigeon, shelduck, pintail and mallard congregate on the water now covering the salt marsh. Look out also for eider and red-breasted merganser, both of which have increased in recent years and the former now breeds on Chapel Island. Long-tailed duck and goosander have also occurred. Check both the tide-line and the fields inland for meadow pipits and especially in winter rock pipits and also reed buntings. The fields may support flocks of lapwing and, at times, golden plover, along with winter thrushes and of course the common farmland birds.

3. *The path follows the sea wall embankment right to West Plain Farm where it rejoins the road. Take care not to leave the embankment especially on the highest of spring tides when almost all the salt marsh will be covered. Frequent stops along this section are recommended from the elevated embankment which affords excellent views.*

After turning the corner at Cowpren Point, check immediately by scanning the marsh where the waders are gathering. They often start at this end of the marsh and then as the tide rises they move along the marsh towards West Plain. A good plan is to position yourself opposite the main wader concentration. These are mainly oystercatcher, curlew, knot, redshank and dunlin, with smaller numbers of bar-tailed godwit and grey plover. With the tide still flowing there is constant movement, especially of the smaller waders which take to the wing as their roost site is made untenable by the rising tide. It is possible to detect when the tide is on the turn for the movement ceases, except of course if a peregrine or merlin launches a sudden attack. Again it is mainly the dunlin, knot and redshank which take to the wing, the larger oystercatcher and curlew treating the attacker with disdain.

The inland fields are at their best when they are flooded following periods of heavy rain. At such times a good selection of waders feed there, their numbers augmented at high tide by large numbers of especially the smaller waders.

Wildfowl include numbers of shelduck, wigeon, pintail and mallard. There is also usually a gull roost, especially of the larger species. The embankment and the inland dyke and fields should be checked for reed buntings and skylarks. Water rails occasionally skulk in the overgrown dyke. At passage periods large numbers of meadow pipits and pied wagtails often pass along the salt marsh. On the seaward side the small pools and flooded areas often attract snipe, while the rushy patches occasionally hold short-eared owls, which take to the wing if flooded out by the tide.

4. *Follow the long straight road from West Plain Farm back to Flookborough, returning either to the car park or Cark and Cartmel railway station.*

The road passes through mainly agricultural land and here again the fields are at their best when flooded. Numbers of oystercatcher and redshank along with lapwing and at times golden plover feed in the fields. They may be joined by flocks of jackdaw and check any stubble fields for flocks of skylarks, finches and buntings.

Pintail

Foulney Island

Arctic Tern.   C.D.

Start: Start and finish at Rampside
Grid reference: 235661
Distance: 5 km (3.1 miles)
Time: Allow up to six hours and aim to be crossing the causeway to Foulney around two to three hours before high tide
Grade: Easy
General: Car parking, toilet and refreshment facilities at Rampside and Roa Island; railway stations at Roose and Barrow; Stagecoach bus service between Ulverston and Barrow
Safety warning: **Carefully study the tide table, for it should be noted that on high tides Foulney Island may be cut off from the mainland**

FOULNEY IS ONE OF FOUR SMALL ISLANDS lying between mainland Furness and the southern tip of Walney Island. Foulney Island is attached to the Roa Island causeway by its own causeway originally built to prevent silting of the Piel channel. The causeway to Roa Island was built by John Abel Smith, who was also responsible for the construction of the pier on Roa Island and ran a steamship service across the bay to Fleetwood during the early Victorian era. In 1852 the whole undertaking was sold to the Furness Railway Company which rebuilt both causeway and pier. The Roa Island railway branch to Barrow crossed the causeway and survived until 1936. There was one intermediate station at Rampside.

The Norse name of Foula suggests long occupation of Foulney Island by

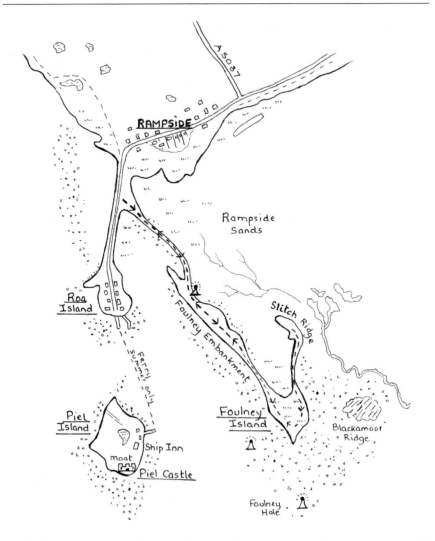

bird colonies. In Domesday, Foulney is referred to as Fugl Ey. In 1292 records from Furness Abbey show that there was an abbey farm or grange nearby known as Rameshede (Rampside) which was known as the grange with the fishery. Furness Abbey owned Piel which, rather confusingly, was known as Foudrey or Fotheray, and may also have owned Foulney. Although Foulney has long been known as a bird island, the earliest bird records come from the 1840s when roseate and common terns nested in roughly equal numbers and little and Arctic terns were also present. In the early years of the Cumbria Trust's involvement, the terns had a series of catastrophic years due to rats being present on the island. In 1965, 200 rats were killed and it was only due to intensive winter baiting that the problem was resolved, allowing a sustained increase in the tern and gull populations.

From the village of Rampside, follow the road towards Roa Island. If arriving by car, park in the small car park on the left hand side of the causeway. From here take the causeway path onto the island path and during the breeding season, please keep to this path to avoid crushing eggs and disturbing nesting birds on the beaches and grasslands. Foulney Island is owned by Broughton Estates and leased to the Cumbria Wildlife Trust which has managed the island as a reserve since appointing its first warden in 1963. The island is uninhabited except by the warden who supervises the reserve during the summer.

The Wild Birds (Foulney) Order, 1980, gives the island legal protection and prevents access to the Slitch Ridge tern colony between 1st April and 15th August each year. Dogs are not permitted on the reserve at all during this period.

Today Foulney is still essentially a bird reserve and during the summer its main conservation interest lies in its breeding terns and nesting shore birds. Tern colonies are fickle and individual species are under considerable pressure for a variety of reasons, including commercialisation of the sand eel industry. The rare roseate tern has only bred sporadically on Foulney since 1963 and, reflecting trends elsewhere, may now be regarded as extinct as a breeding species on the island. Common tern, sandwich tern and associated

C.Dodding.

Piel Castle and Eiders

black-headed gulls have not nested on Foulney since the mid 1990s. Mussel beds just offshore make it, along with South Walney, an ideal breeding place for eiders which nested on Foulney for the first time in 1965. Their numbers gradually increased and peaked in 1993 with 297 pairs.[1] However, during 2004, there were only about 30 pairs of Britain's heaviest and fastest flying sea duck nesting on Foulney. Eiders are an endearing species especially during spring when the courtship display of the male can be seen and heard around the island. Several males will often serenade one female by throwing their heads back and making their fabulous cooing calls. Female eiders are renowned for their courage in sitting tightly on their eggs but if disturbed will abandon the nest. Arctic terns and the endangered little tern continue to utilise Foulney as a safe supervised haven for nesting and during 2005 the colonies were showing signs of recovering after a run of poor years. Other important species present during 2005 included about 100 pairs of oyster-catcher, 20 pairs of ringed plover and 7 pairs of skylark.

As the terns leave Foulney in late summer with their newly fledged young, thousands of waders and wildfowl make their southward journey here to winter. Foulney and its surrounding inter-tidal areas provide a feeding and roosting area for curlew, bar-tailed godwit, knot, grey plover, dunlin and oystercatcher. Peregrine and merlin regularly pursue the roosting wader flocks while short-eared owl and kestrel hunt for small mammals in the long grass. A small party of dark-bellied brent geese has been present each winter for many years. They come to feed on the zostera or scare eelgrass, on the inter-tidal area. During the autumn and winter months, cormorant, eider and common scoter can be seen roosting during high tide along the beach off Slitch Ridge. Winter visitors seen from Foulney's shingle have included great crested grebe, Slavonian grebe, black-necked grebe, goldeneye, shelduck, wigeon, red-breasted merganser, red-throated diver, long-tailed duck, razorbill, guillemot and glaucous gull, snow bunting, brambling, twite and shore lark.

Spring and autumn passage have produced black-tailed godwit, sanderling, little stint, curlew sandpiper, jack snipe, whimbrel, spotted redshank, green-shank, roseate tern, black tern, Mediterranean gull, little gull and great and Arctic skua. Notable rarities are represented by sightings of bluethroat, hobby, temminck's stint, ring-billed gull, pomarine skua and during May, 2004, three spoonbills landed to the obvious delight of the warden. Excep-tionally a bridled tern appeared in the tern colony for three days in June 1994.

South Walney and Foulney comprise one of the best areas of vegetated shingle in Britain. Above the high water mark is a zone of bare shingle

---

1   *Cumbrian Wildlife* No. 59

with scattered plants of sea kale, yellow-horned poppy, curled dock and sea campion. Unfortunately the nationally rare oyster plant has not been recorded on Foulney since 1975. Diversity increases with distance from the sea and birds' foot trefoil, biting stonecrop, herb Robert and scurvy grass complement the ground flora. Salt marsh is developing in the bay between the main island and Slitch Ridge and on the eastern side of the causeway, with cord grass becoming more widespread.

Foulney has interesting populations of butterflies and moths. Grayling, red admiral, large and small white, meadow brown, common blue, small copper and six-spot burnet are regularly recorded; the latter sometimes in thousands. In 1986 five hummingbird hawk-moths were recorded feeding on thistle on the island. In recent years, grey seals have become quite numerous in this part of Morecambe Bay and although their regular haul out is the spit at South Walney, Foulney provides the best view point, particularly in June and July. Other interesting offshore sightings observed from Foulney have included porpoise and basking shark. Voles and shrews make their home in the long grassland at the western end of the island and keep active throughout the year. Brown rats have not been recorded since being eradicated but other mammalian predators have included stoat, weasel and hedgehog. The ternary is also predated by foxes which walk across the mud flats at night to target ground nesting birds and generally create havoc!

Sea kale on Foulney. In the background in Roa Island (photo by D. Hindle)

The Greenway to Roa Island
via Cavendish Dock

Sedge Warbler.

Start: Start at Roose railway station or Cavendish
Dock and finish at Roa Island
Grid reference: SD218687 (Cavendish Dock)
Distance: 7 km (4.3 miles) one way
Time: Five hours
Grade: Easy
General: Parking, toilet and refreshment facilities at
Rampside and Roa Island; railway stations at
Roose and Barrow

Cumbria's 'Greenway', part of the Cumbria Coastal Way, leads from its
industrial shipbuilding heartland at Cavendish Dock along the course
of an old railway line past the modern Roosecote Power Station and Barrow
Onshore Gas Terminal to the village of Rampside. The final section of the
walk crosses the road causeway linking the Furness Peninsula with Roa
Island. The Furness Railway Company originally built their railway to Roa
Island in an almost straight line linking Barrow with Roa Island to ship out
slate and iron ore. The high embankment now affords good bird watching,
with views of the channel separating Walney with its landmark white lighthouse and Piel Island with its mediaeval ruined castle which once belonged
to the monks of Furness Abbey. The most productive time to commence this
walk is approximately three hours before a nine-metre high tide.

1. *Study the bus and train timetables for this walk utilises public transport – outward by train to Roose Station and return Stagecoach bus from Roa Island to either Roose or Barrow railway station. To reach Cavendish Dock and the start of the walk leave Roose Station and turn right along the main road towards Barrow. Take the first turning left and walk through the housing estate, taking two left turns and proceeding under the railway line to Cavendish Dock.*

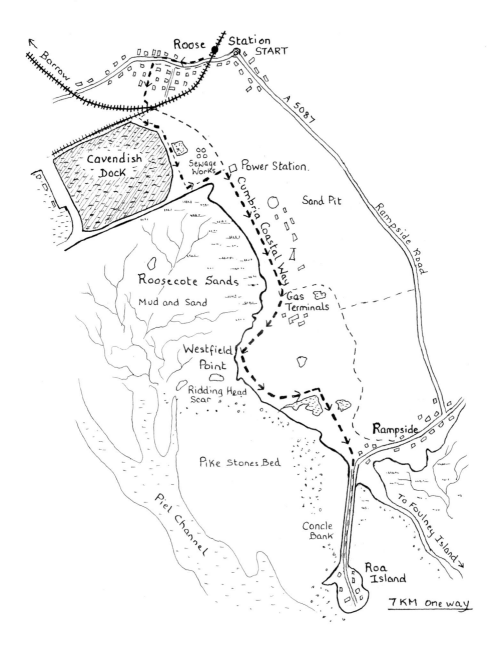

Commence serious birding from the wall demarcating the north-east corner of Cavendish Dock and gradually walk round to the south-west side. The water in Cavendish Dock is two to three degrees warmer than the other docks and attracts large numbers of waterfowl, waders, terns, gulls and some rarities. The dock is a large cooling reservoir for the nearby Roosecote power station and when the air is cold the water steams and the exit pipe takes on an almost surreal appearance with its rows of perching cormorants, redshank and dunlin.

Flocks of black-headed, herring, lesser and greater black-backed gulls, coot and over a hundred mute swans are often present. Post breeding dispersal leads to increased numbers of coot in autumn and winter when great crested grebe are commonly seen, while a few little grebe feed near the edges. In winter look out for scattered groups of diving ducks, including red breasted merganser, goosander, goldeneye, tufted duck and pochard and occasional scaup and long-tailed duck. As distinct from the diving ducks, surface feeding ducks such as wigeon, teal, mallard and shoveler may also be observed on the open water.

Seasonal passage and storms have produced Slavonian, red-necked and black-necked grebe, and red-throated, black-throated, great northern diver and occasional black tern and little gull. Cavendish Dock has been frequented by several rarities. Over the years a distinguished cast has included ferruginous duck, temminck's stint, pectoral sandpiper, spotted sandpiper, avocet, lesser yellowlegs, white-winged black tern, woodlark, water pipit and Lapland bunting.

2. *Walk along the side of the dock to the south-east corner and proceed left towards Roosecote power station and right along Greenway, passing the onshore gas terminal and Westfield Point to Rampside, a distance of approximately four kilometres. Ahead is the road causeway connecting with Roa Island marking the end of the walk.*

View the mudflats at Roosecote Sands on a rising tide from the wall or causeway that runs along the southern side of the dock. This is an important site for wildfowl and waders and in winter flocks of eider, wigeon, mallard, teal and shelduck occur at high tide. Feeding flocks of dunlin, knot, redshank, curlew, bar-tailed godwit, oystercatcher, ringed, grey and golden plover move to the salt marsh at high tide. Passage migrants such as whimbrel and greenshank may be seen during spring and autumn passage. Near the power station, is Salthouse Pool, an attractive phragmities reed-fringed habitat, suitable for mallard, teal, moorhen, and typical reed bed birds such as snipe, water rail, heron, sedge warbler and reed bunting,

Peregrine falcons have adapted to nesting on artificial, man-made industrial structures such as the power station, which also provides a good look-out post. Opportunistic peregrines, merlin and sparrowhawks may be

great crested grebe

seen pursuing the wader flocks and smaller birds. Almost anywhere on this walk is a good place to see resident stonechat, song thrush, kestrel, linnet, goldfinch and smaller numbers of redpoll. Passage migrants include white wagtails and wheatear. Flocks of fieldfares and redwings devour the winter crop of the hawthorn's bright red berries and single rock pipits may also be seen in winter frequenting the tide-line. Also during the winter months kingfishers may travel widely to find areas of unfrozen water and at such times the coast and areas like Cavendish Dock are favoured.

Hydrocarbon Resources Ltd has established the onshore gas terminal covering over twenty hectares of land close to Westfield Point and the facilities are expected to process gas throughout the forty year life of the Morecambe Bay gas field. The terminal is built in a natural hollow and landscaped with several thousand trees, shrubs and ponds fringed with reed, willow and reed beds visible from a nature trail which is well worth a diversionary walk from Greenway. The Westfield nature trails highlight these wildlife habitats with good biodiversity, including spawning pools for frogs, toads and newts. The endangered water vole also occurs here and is now afforded special protection under the provisions of the Wildlife and Countryside Act, 1981.

Check the extensive cover and hedgerows for sheltering migrants in spring and autumn. The Westfield trail harbours both rare and common warbler species such as whitethroat, lesser whitethroat, garden warbler, willow warbler, sedge warbler and grasshopper warbler. In fields close to Westfield Point there are several dykes with reedy areas and a pool where snipe may be seen feeding before flying off with characteristic zigzag flight and harsh 'ketsch' calls. The pool is the haunt of greylag geese, mute swan, coot, moorhen, wigeon, teal, snipe, redshank, greenshank and reed bunting.

Offshore at Westfield Point is Ridding Head Scar, a shingle bank projecting out into Roosecote Sands. The scar is one of the last areas to be submerged by the rising tide. It is used as a roosting area by wading birds such as oystercatcher, redshank, curlew, bar-tailed godwit, ringed, grey and golden plover. At Rampside it is important to check the mudflats for small parties of wintering brent geese before crossing the causeway to Roa Island and observing the birds of the Walney channel, further described in the Walney Island walk. Mussel beds occur on rocky scars in the intertidal area around the islands and are a major attraction for eiders and several species of wader. If time permits do not forget to contact the ferryman and explore Piel Island. It is possible to reach the castle and the King of Piel, who is known to frequent the Ship Inn, by telephoning the ferryman on 01229 835809. After partaking of a jar or two of the local brew and meeting the King in the Ship Inn your day's list should increase tenfold!

The nationally scarce oyster plant was last recorded at Foulney in 1975 and on South Walney nature reserve in 1976 (photo D. Hindle)

South Walney Nature Reserve

Eider.   C.D.

Start: Starts and finishes at the reserve car park
Grid reference: SD204633
Distance: 7 km (4.3 miles) Reserve area only
Time: Allow 4 to 6 hours
Grade: Easy
General: Toilets at the car park other facilities in Barrow-in-Furness
Wheelchair access to gate pond hide, check with the warden to see if other tracks are suitable. Disabled toilets

THIS WALK PROVIDES EXCELLENT BIRD WATCHING all year round. It takes in the sand dunes and gravel pits of the reserve, all set against the ever-changing world of the tidal regime. The walk concentrates on the reserve with its excellent facilities of paths and hides, but a possible extension for those wanting a longer walk is included. Watching is at its best when the tide is above 8.5 metres and it is best to arrive at least two hours before high tide.

1. *Park in the reserve car park and obtain your day permit from the kiosk. An information board gives details of recent sightings. Take the well marked trail down the inner side of the island towards the pier hide overlooking Lighthouse Bay.*

During the breeding season from February to early August the numbers of large gulls is somewhat overwhelming to first time visitors. Old hands know to wear old clothes and a hat, for you never know what they will drop on you! The breeding population has recently been estimated at about 30,000 pairs, of which lesser black-backed gulls make up two thirds and herring gulls the rest, except for about eighty pairs of great black-backed gulls. It is a stimulating experience to walk through the colony with the gulls rising

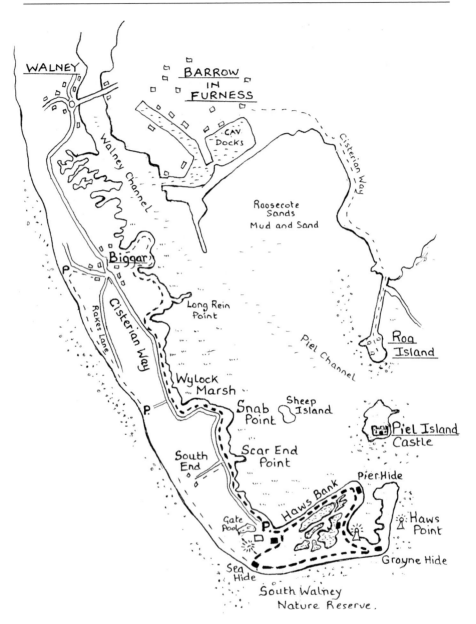

before you and quickly settling behind you, the cacophony of sound and the smell adding to the experience. May and June are the best times to visit for you can see nests at all stages of development. A clue to the food preferences of the birds can be gained from the remains around the nest, some specialising on prey from the inter-tidal area while others clearly prefer to visit the rubbish tips of Barrow! You will have no problem seeing the two common species for they are everywhere. The greater black-backs prefer the islands and spits within the gravel pit complex, their much darker mantles and larger size making them clearly recognisable.

Nesting among the gulls are large numbers of eiders. At one time up to 1500 pairs nested at Walney but predation by foxes and possibly over-exploitation by man of their main food source, mussels, has caused a decline to around 300 pairs in recent years. From late winter through to early spring rafts of birds float offshore. The highly colourful males court the drab females with much head bobbing and jerking, delivering the lovely cooing note. As the season progresses and most females are incubating, the display gets even more frantic as several males surround each still unpaired female in a bid to win her favours. In the groups are many adolescent males, not in full plumage and not old enough to breed.

They nest on the ground among vegetation or tidal debris and some can be quite exposed with the female undertaking all the incubation. When hatched the young are led onto the sea and here the ducklings mix with other broods to form crèches in an attempt to protect them from marauding gulls.

During the walk along the shore, scan the flocks of oystercatchers, curlew, dunlin and redshank which are eventually pushed off by the rising tide when they flight towards the high tide roosts at the south of the Island or to Sheep Island to the north. Numbers of ringed plover and turnstone roost at high tide along the shingle beaches. Redshank and dunlin will also roost there

C. Dodding.

South Walney
Lighthouse

but are much more likely to leave as you approach. On the flowing tide large flocks of eiders and shelduck, along with red-breasted mergansers, also head toward the spit at the south of the island. In winter the sand dunes often hold flocks of twite and other finches, including goldfinch and linnet.

In spring and summer look out for South Walney's special plants, many of them extremely colourful and with intriguing names such as henbane, viper's bugloss, hound's tongue, mullein and yellow-horned poppy along with the delightful wild pansy which flowers from May until November.

To the west of the track are the old gravel workings and the oyster farm. The water areas, islands and spits hold grebes wildfowl, especially merganser and goldeneye but also surface feeding ducks such as wigeon, shoveler and teal and waders such as greenshank and spotted redshank

The pier hide looks out towards the distant Piel and Foulney Islands. In the foreground the entrance to Lighthouse Bay and the large spit which forms the south of the island. Here at high tide congregate large numbers of oyster-catcher and eiders along with smaller numbers of grey plover, sanderling, turnstone, knot, dunlin, cormorant, wigeon and a motley collection of gulls. Careful watching of the bay and the water towards Piel Island usually reveals red-throated and occasionally other divers along with great crested grebes and common scoter, with the odd long-tailed ducks and scaup. Watch out for the ravens which now breed and frequent Piel Castle.

2. *Leaving the hide as the tide ebbs, head along the path past the lighthouse and out to the groyne hide then back and to the sea hide.*

Here one can view both the Walney Channel and the Irish Sea and watch for birds passing along the coast, including terns, sea duck, waders and wildfowl. Peregrines and merlins are regular, often disturbing the roosting waders and providing a superb spectacle. The walk towards the sea hide takes you through the densest part of the gullery and is also a good area for nesting eiders. In winter short-eared owl frequent the grassy areas, as do twite and occasionally small parties of snow bunting.

The sea hide, as its name suggests, is ideal for sea watching in comfort. Winds with a westerly element produce the best results but patience is needed and you can then be rewarded with sights of gannets, kittiwakes, fulmars, guillemot, razor bill, red-throated divers, Arctic terns, Manx shear-water, great and Arctic skuas, common and velvet scoters and occasionally Leach's and storm petrels.

3. *From the sea hide, head back towards the car park but take the diversion to the hide which overlooks Gate Pond before returning to the car park.*

The Gate Pond hide gives a good chance of seeing freshwater waders such as snipe, ruff and black-tailed godwit, and wildfowl including shoveler, gadwall and teal. You are never quite certain what might turn up; for example there are several records of grey phalarope on this small pool.

The bushes round the cottages and kiosk are well worth checking, although you need to be a member of the Walney Bird Observatory to drive the Heligoland trap. An amazing variety of passerines have been recorded over the years at South Walney, from bluethroat to melodious warbler. The highlight though was the third record for the country of a white-throated sparrow.

4. *Depending on the time of year and of course what birds are present, a visit to South Walney can take the best part of a day, but for those who want to explore further it is possible to take the road and public footpaths along the sea shore to reach the small hamlet of Biggar Bank then cross the island and return to South Walney along the Irish Sea coast. This is the longer walk and a shorter walk is also shown on the map, taking in the fields and seashore just outside the reserve.*

On the longer walk, high tide wader and wildfowl roosts can be found at Bent How, Scar End and Snab Points. Species composition is similar to South Walney but Bent How can be good for sanderling and small numbers of purple sandpipers. The hedges and gorse clumps attract breeding stonechat and linnets and at passage periods look out for migrant wheatear, whinchat and warblers. The many fields or patches of rough grass still attract skylarks and at migration times flocks of meadow pipits and, when flooded, wildfowl and waders. Twite and linnets regularly frequent the rough ground and coast line in winter, as occasionally do small parties of snow buntings.

5. *It is possible to visit the Cavendish Dock area on the way home. For details see walk 23.*

The Walney geranium is a pale pink subspecies of Bloody Cranesbill bestowed with the Latin name of Geranium Sangineum Lancastriense thus mirroring its unique status and distribution in the former red rose county.
(photo by D. Hindle)

The Duddon challenger

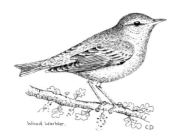

Wood Warbler.   CD

Start: Start and finish at SD192897
Distance: 10 km (6.2 miles)
Time: Allow 5 hours
Grade: Easy to moderate
General: Toilet and refreshment facilities at Broughton, Post Office/shop at Ulpha; only limited parking near starting point. Nearest unmanned railway station at Foxfield

A CIRCULAR WALK ALONG THE UNSPOILT lower Duddon Valley, embracing magnificent scenery, an abundance of wild flowers and habitat diversity. The approach is fundamentally different from the preceding walks in that no clues as to likely species are given. The challenge is to record your own list of birds to be found within a typical south Lakeland valley. A careful, observant approach in late April or early May should reveal one or two surprises. Good birding!

This valley was William Wordsworth's 'long loved valley,' and Ulpha's ancient church, reached through a lych-gate, would have been known to him. The ghostly ruins of Frith Hall, standing prominently forlorn and not surprisingly reputedly haunted, were originally used as a pack horse station before being used as an inn. In one of several Duddon sonnets Wordsworth sums up Frith Hall:

> Fallen, and diffused into a shapeless heap,
> Or quietly self-buried in earth's mould,
> Is that embattled house, whose massy keep,
> Flung from yon cliff a shadow large and cold,
> There dwelt the gay, the bountiful, the bold ...

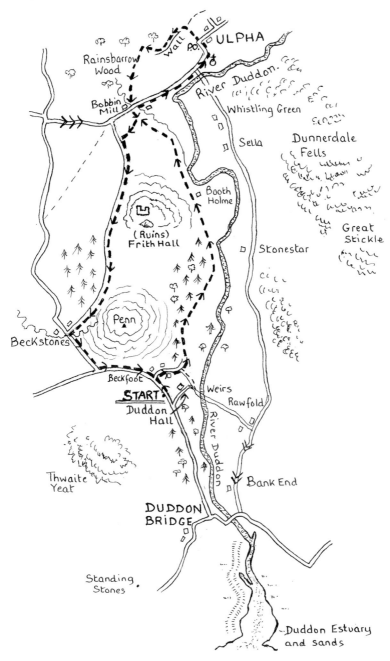

We do not think you will be ticking off any ghosts, only birds, but when passing Frith Hall just think about 'that embattled house' and your imagination may run riot and conjure up something, if only a ghostly barn owl!

1. *At Duddon Bridge take the road immediately to the west of the river towards Corney Fell. After one mile and passing Duddon Hall, take the track right by following the sign indicating Broughton Mill and Ulpha. Ignore the footpath to Rowfold Bridge and keep left through Forge Wood. At a gate the track leaves the wood and skirts a field before going onto a lane. Keep straight on to arrive at the bobbin mills. Turn right along the road and at Ulpha Bridge fork left to have a look at the church and post office/shop.*

2. *At the post office corner go through a gate and proceed left to another gate between the wall and Rainsbarrow Wood which widens to a woodland track, bedecked by several wood ant hills, to arrive back at the bobbin mill. Turn right over the bridge and then immediately left through the gate. Follow the path taking the right hand fork uphill and proceed through a gate to Bleabeck Bridge and follow the track past the ruins of Frith Hall. Proceed through the forestry plantation of Ulpha Park. After a short distance where the forestry plantation on the left finishes, there is a wall stile that may provide an opportunity to see a few more birds by giving access to the small fell of Penn and some superb views. Regain the main track which continues downhill between the plantation and the wall through a gate to the road at Beckstones. Cross over the cascading Logan Beck by the bridge and follow the road to the junction. Keep left, over the cattle grid and descend the hill to the starting point.*

How many birds? Depending on time of year and provided you are tuned into calls and songs, a total of 40 to 50 species is probable, plus a thoroughly enjoyable walk in southern lakeland.

Frith Hall (Ruins)
Duddon Valley

C. Dodding.

'The Green Road' to Millom

Shelduck. N B

Start: Start at Green Road railway station and finish at Millom station

Grid reference: 190840

Distance: 5.5 km (3.4 miles) one way

Time: Allow 3 to 4 hours

Grade: Easy

General: Toilet and refreshment facilities are available at Millom. Tourist Information at Millom railway station. Limited parking at Green Road unmanned railway station

THIS IS AN EASY WALK BETWEEN Green Road and Millom Railway Stations, offering good views of the estuary while walking along an elevated embankment overlooking Millom Marsh. It is preferable to do the walk on an incoming tide of at least nine metres in order to obtain closer views of wildfowl and waders both on the marshes and in the channels.

1. *Travelling by car Green Road station is reached by following a minor road from the village of The Green, situated south of the hamlet of The Hill. From the level crossing at Green Road station walk right along a minor lane to Millom Marsh. Turn right onto the embankment – part of the 'Cumbria Coastal Way' and follow it for about four kilometres to reach Lancashire Road, Millom. To return to Green Road, catch a train at Millom Station (infrequent service) or walk back along the embankment.*

The Duddon estuary comprises salt marshes, sands and the main river channel, shadowed by the distinctive landmark of Black Combe. The estuary extends from Duddon railway viaduct to Dunnerholme and Sandscale Haws

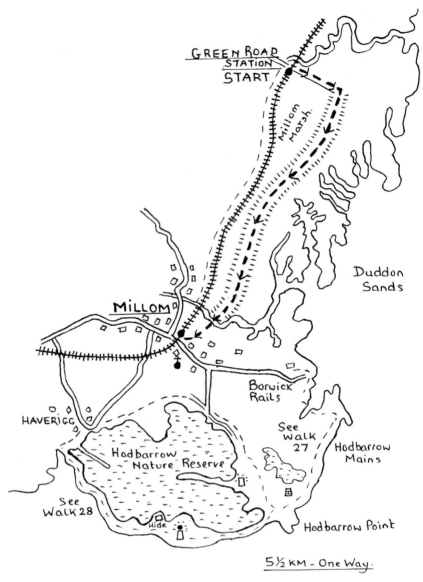

GREEN ROAD
STATION
START

Millom Marsh

Duddon
Sands

MILLOM

Borwick
Rails

HAVERIGG

See
walk
27

Hodbarrow
Mains

Hodbarrow
Nature Reserve

See
Walk 28

Hide

Hodbarrow Point

5½ KM – One Way.

on the south side and the town of Millom and Haverigg Point on the north side. The primitive west Cumbria railway takes a meandering course around the Duddon estuary serving the smallest of communities. Not surprisingly, when the railway was built there were plans for a bridge across the Duddon estuary that never materialised. Miraculously the line managed to escape Dr. Beeching's closure programme in the 1960s and evidently the authorities of Network Rail have still not caught up with it. To disembark at Green Road Station it is necessary to inform the guard.

On Millom Marsh look out for greylag geese with smaller numbers of pink-footed geese. At the right time of year expect also pintail, wigeon, teal, red-breasted merganser, mallard, cormorant, golden plover, oystercatcher, redshank, curlew, whimbrel, ringed plover, dunlin, black-tailed godwit, and greenshank. Smaller birds are worthy of attention and flocks of chaffinch, greenfinch, goldfinch and a few reed bunting may be present. During winter care should be taken with the identification of rock pipit and meadow pipit and twite and linnet, for all these confusing species also occur. One of the best aids to identification is to listen for their characteristic calls. Waders and wildfowl flock add to the natural sounds that undoubtedly reflect the character of the estuary and salt marsh, before we reach the urban environment of Millom with its resident collared doves.

Collared dove

Wednesday, early closing:
birds and heritage at Millom

Stonechat

Start:	Start and finish at Millom railway station
Grid reference:	SD172802
Distance:	7 km (4.3 miles)
Time:	Four hours
Grade:	Easy
General:	Toilet, parking and refreshment facilities are available at Millom. Tourist Information at Millom railway station where town maps may be obtained

MILLOM IS A SMALL TOWN WITH NEAT ROWS of terraced houses and period shops in streets buzzing with friendly people. The Lakeland poet and author, Norman Nicholson, was born and bred here and a blue plaque marks number 14, St George's Terrace where he resided for most of his working life. One of his books about Millom was entitled *Wednesday, Early Closing*, and it still is so do not forget if you need the shops. Millom Iron Works was the town's principal employer until its closure in 1968. Nowadays, the town is transferring its allegiance from its industrial past to tourism, including the provision of facilities for observing wildlife and bird watching. The local museum and tourist information centre now occupy several rooms at Millom railway station and are well worth a visit. It is preferable to do the walk on an incoming tide of at least nine metres in order to obtain closer views of wildfowl and waders, both on the marshes and in the channels.

1. *From the south end of Millom railway station north-bound platform take the properly constructed path turning left into Lancashire Road. At the end of Lancashire Road gain the Cumbria Coastal Way. Where the footpath diverges after a short distance, take the right fork east along a narrow path that broadens into a track to reach the site of Millom Iron Works and its legacy of a nature reserve. Alternatively to experience the flavour of Millom seek out a town centre route via busy Wellington Street and Albert Street and Albert Street to the iron works reserve. At the top of the old slag heap there is a well placed seat and a toposcope that describes the panorama of the western fells featuring England's highest mountain, 'Scafell'. Continue along the path to the old pier at Borwick Rails keeping right along the Cumbria Coastal Way. Walk across Hodbarrow Mains and over the headland at Hodbarrow Point to the RSPB nature reserve. With the main lagoon and the sea wall on your left take a right hand track that leads away from the Cumbria Coastal Way through the old mining area. Skirt the reserve before turning right onto Mainsgate Road and return to Millom Station by turning left into St George's Road.*

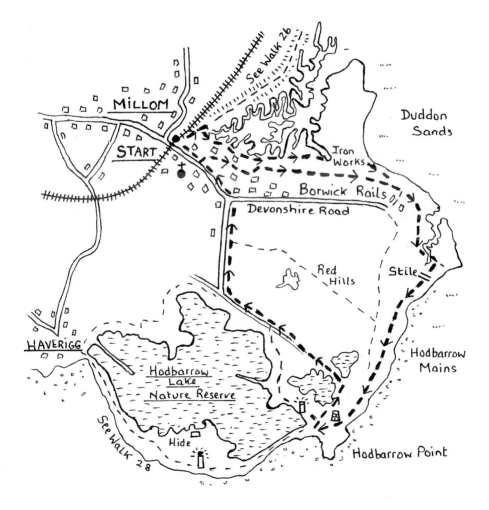

The Iron Works Local Nature Reserve and Borwick Rails pier exemplify how land reclamation of a former major industrial site can be put to excellent use and enhance biodiversity. The site has reverted to nature and plant communities have developed on the slag and disturbed ground, typically represented by bee orchids and yellow wort, while the grasslands host several species of butterfly. Rare amphibians are represented by natterjack toads. These engaging creatures breed in several pools where dragonflies hawk over the water during the summer months looking to lay their eggs.

Today the old harbour at Borwick Rails plays host to birds rather than the Victorian sailing ships that plied their trade and the more recent Royal Navy ships that came here to be scrapped. The site provides excellent views of the estuary across to Dunnerholme, Sandscale and Walney Island, seen against a backcloth of the hills of the Furness peninsula and the mountains of south and west Cumbria. Again the tide is crucial and although birds are more active on a rising tide, high and low tide offer something different. Have lunch at the top of the slag heap for if you have planned it right, by now the tide will have started to ebb and there will be both water and exposed mud. The reserve attracts warblers, rock pipit, meadow pipit, stonechat and skylark while the on-site summit viewpoint provides a good watch point for resident and passage sea birds, wildfowl, waders and terns. The Duddon channel and mudflats are the haunt of redshank, spotted redshank, green-shank, curlew, oystercatcher, lapwing, dunlin, knot, common sandpiper, godwits, red-breasted merganser, mallard, pintail, goldeneye, teal, wigeon, eider, great crested grebe, cormorant, heron and occasional red-throated diver, guillemot and razorbill.

In spring expect to see both the smallest (little tern) and largest member of the tern family (sandwich tern) as well as common and the occasional Arctic tern, often euphemistically known as 'comic terns' or perhaps more elegantly, sea swallows. Up to four species of tern may be seen flying to and from the breeding colony at Hodbarrow. With any luck the young birds from this colony will have fledged by the end of June and be on the wing, thus presenting a few more identification challenges.

The walk between Millom and Hodbarrow can be rewarding and, depending on time of year, offers ringed plover, dunlin, oystercatcher, whimbrel, curlew, whitethroat, garden warbler, willow warbler, grasshopper warbler, wheatear, stonechat, reed bunting, skylark, rock pipit, meadow pipit, stonechat, kestrel, merlin, peregrine falcon and sparrow hawk.

Millom and Hodbarrow Mains and Hodbarrow Point known locally as 'The Rocks', is good for migrants taking advantage of the diversity of small cliffs, foreshore, scrub, copses and the large lagoon that is integral to the R.S.P.B.'s Hodbarrow Nature Reserve. The reserve, (see walk 28) is the flooded site of a former iron ore mine and is enclosed by a sea wall built over a hundred

Industrial archaeology at Millom, c1968–70 (formerly the haunt of breeding barn owls) before the pumps were turned off and the mine workings flooded, which gave birth to the large lagoon at the RSPB Hodbarrow Reserve. (photo by D. Hindle)

years ago. Most of the industrial archaeology was removed in the 1970/80s, but two lighthouse towers and the walls of a windmill remain. Near the stump of an old windmill the cliffs at Hodbarrow Point are worth exploring at low tide for they are home to that localised but hardy maritime fern, the sea spleenwort.

Today the reserve fulfils important criteria as a site for passage of wildfowl and waders and as a breeding site for them. The main lagoon and smaller meres are now home to many species of waterfowl, including large numbers of red-breasted merganser and thousands of waders in autumn and winter. Of particular importance, however, is the specially protected tern colony that hosts up to four of the five British species. The reserve can be viewed while walking round it or from a hide located on the sea wall which is open all year.

Millom and Hodbarrow circular

Little Tern. C.D.

Start: Start and finish Millom railway station
Grid reference: SD172802
Distance: 6.5 km (4 miles)
Time: Allow 5 to 6 hours
Grade: Easy
General: Toilets, refreshments and other services are available in Millom. Car park available on the reserve, follow the brown tourist information signs in Millom

THIS RSPB RESERVE HAS SO MUCH to offer throughout the year, although probably is at its best from late April to early July. The wide range of habitats and ease of access allow a full day's birding without too much walking. Visits timed to coincide with high tide are probably best but there is always plenty to see. This walk can be undertaken either from Millom railway station or by car, with parking available on the side of the track at the start of the sea wall but take care, the track is rather rough.

1. *Turn left out of the railway station and then left and over the bridge along Millom's main street and follow the brown tourist signs to the RSPB reserve. The reserve starts as the water comes into view so take the left turn onto the rough track.*

On this walk through the small town look out for house martins and swifts and house sparrows which are still common here. The large water area is visible on the right and good views are possible through gaps in the fringeing willows. This usually reveals numbers of great crested grebe, pochard and tufted duck, and in winter goldeneye, along with large numbers of coot.

2. *Take the first footpath on the right, which takes you on a loop through the willow, birch and gorse scrub, eventually coming out near the sea wall parking place. There are several other side paths between the lagoon and the main track which are well worth exploring, including paths which take you to two small lagoons, one deep the other shallow. In good weather in spring, allow up to two hours to explore this area.*

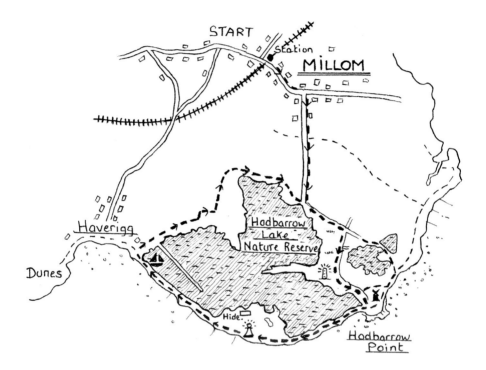

The scrub areas are excellent for breeding warblers with good numbers of whitethroat, willow, sedge and garden warblers, chiffchaff, blackcap and the two less common species, grasshopper warbler and lesser whitethroat. It is an excellent place to learn or brush up on your song identification! You will notice subtle differences in the habitats of these warblers, with chiffchaff, blackcap and lesser whitethroat mainly in the more mature areas of scrub and the others in the shorter, bushier areas. Other common breeders include reed bunting and linnet. In season this area is excellent botanically, including northern marsh, pyramidal and bee orchids which flower in June and early July.

The deep lagoon is good for both surface feeding and diving duck. The shallow lagoon on the south of the main track is excellent for little grebe, greylag, teal and, at passage periods, freshwater waders including green sandpiper and greenshank. Natterjack toads breed in several of the smaller pools. This general area and the fields to the south of the track are well used by barn owl, mainly at dawn and dusk but especially in winter they can be seen hunting at any time of day. The extensive tracts of gorse are regularly favoured by stonechats.

3. *Return to the car parking area and take the track along the sea wall towards the hide, which overlooks the lagoon and the large island.*

From here on you have views over both the estuary on one side and the lagoon on the other. If you time your arrival to coincide with the incoming tide you can watch flocks of oystercatchers, dunlin, knot, redshank and bar-tailed godwits passing close to you as they seek refuge on the high tide roosts. With them are flocks of duck, especially shelduck, wigeon, eider and merganser. The spectacle is best from late autumn to early spring but there is always something to see. When the tide is in, watch out for seabirds including gannets and skuas; these are usually well out to sea so a telescope is essential. During the breeding season there is a constant passage of terns from the sea to the lagoon, many carrying sand eels which in spring are presented to the female by the males – the avian equivalent of a box of chocolates! The raucous call of the gull-like sandwich tern is heard constantly and the delightfully light and acrobatic flight of the little tern is a joy to watch. Meadow pipits and wheatears often flit in front of you. Botanically the inner part of the sea wall is very interesting with many common limestone plants, including dark red helleborine and pyramidal orchid.

On the approach to the hide watch out for breeding ringed plover and the gorse bushes just past the hide are probably the most favoured stonechat area. The island and water in front of the hide is usually full of birds. In spring the terns take pride of place, especially the densely packed sandwich terns, with the common and the occasional Arctic tern spread more thinly. Right in front of the hide are the delightful little terns, initially difficult to pick out on the bare shingle areas. A careful count though will usually produce between 30 and 50 pairs. The best spectacle is when a 'dread' occurs, sometimes caused by a potential predator and at other times for no apparent reason. This causes all the terns to take to flight and vent their vocal concern in a short lived cacophony of sound. The amount of activity depends on the time of your visit in relation to the breeding cycle. Early in the season there is much displaying as pairs and territories are established. This is followed by a quieter period as incubation takes place. Then, as the young hatch, there is a period of constant to-ing and fro-ing with food for the young birds, culminating in the fledging of many young birds in a successful season.

Other breeding birds include lapwing, ringed plover, redshank, oystercatcher, lesser black-backed and herring gulls, eider, tufted duck, merganser and greylag. Several pairs of great crested grebe build nests which are a great mound of water weed and other debris, scorning any vegetation cover. A pair usually nests in the channel right in front of the hide and the regular building up of the nest can be watched, along with the change-over during incubation. After hatching, try to count the bizarrely striped young as they hitch a ride on their parents' backs. In spring watch out for little gulls hawking insects over the water and easterly winds can bring an influx of black terns.

Waders regularly feed on the muddy margins or use the island as a high tide roost. These are mainly estuarine waders with the best variety during spring and autumn passage periods. Dunlin, knot, redshank, turnstone, ringed plover and black-tailed godwit are the commonest but ruff, green sandpiper, greenshank and spotted redshank are regular in small numbers.

Numbers of wildfowl are always present, especially diving ducks which favour the deeper water. Mergansers use the lagoon as a moulting site in summer, although numbers are somewhat lower than in former years when up to 350 were regular. Of the surface feeders wigeon and teal are the commonest but gadwall, shoveler and pintail are less frequent. The proximity to the sea means that sea duck, especially scaup and common scoter, are fairly regular. During passage periods almost anything may drop in, including both wild swans and brent and barnacle geese.

First time visitors to the hide will be intrigued by the large wall across part of the lagoon, which has obviously been breached at sometime. This wall was built in 1880 to protect the hematite iron ore mine which was one of the richest deposits of iron ore in the country. For *c.* 120 years iron ore was mined and in 1871, 482 people worked on extracting the ore which was kept dry by constant pumping, and at the peak of the industry around 1000 men worked in the mine and the associated iron works. The wall was not fully successful and it was replaced by the present sea wall which was completed in 1905. Looking over the present peaceful scene it is hard to imagine the hive of activity that continued until 1968. Once pumping stopped the lagoon was created, so what we see today is a haven for nature born out of industry. Full details of the history of the area can be found on the very detailed display panels by the recently restored lighthouse on the sea wall behind the hide. It is well worth a read.

4. *Continue along the sea wall until the water ski bank comes into view, then take the first track right down below the sea wall. Return to the sea wall and continue until the end then follow the road to the right along the edge of the caravan site and past the Commodore Hotel and back to the road junction which leads to Millom. This gives a circular walk but the bird watching is less interesting and if birding is your main interest retracing the route back via the sea wall and hide will give the best results.*

The ski bank is the alternative breeding site for the sandwich terns, although at the time of writing the colony has moved to the island in front of the hide. The bank though has been used more than the island in recent years. Sandwich terns are rather fickle in their choice of nest site and often move location after a bad breeding season. Black-headed gulls nest every year on this bank and seem oblivious to any water skiing activities. The scrubby bushes below the sea wall usually have singing sedge warbler and whitethroat.

Watching the estuary from the top of the sea wall gives a good view of the main low tide feeding areas which are good for shore waders and wildfowl. Terns often sit on the exposed sand banks at low water. It is still possible to check for birds on the lagoon although this is the most disturbed part of the area. The scrub areas on the final section of the walk support a similar variety of warblers to the first area visited.

Birds of heath and shore:
Silecroft circular

N.B.

Start: Start and finish at Silecroft railway station
Grid reference: 130820
Distance: 6 km (3.7 miles)
Time: Allow five hours
Grade: Easy to moderate
General: Car parking toilet and refreshment facilities at Silecroft

THIS CIRCULAR WALK COMMENCES and finishes at Silecroft, passing fragments of lowland coastal heath, and provides an opportunity to watch sea birds and experience exhilarating seascapes with distant views of the Isle of Man. The most productive time to commence walking is approximately three hours before high tide.

1. *Arriving by train, alight at the unmanned Silecroft station by informing the guard in advance. On arrival walk along the road through the village to the shore. Depending on the state of the tide either walk south along the sands or alternatively along a footpath between the caravan park and the beach to regain the beach. Walk beyond the Silecroft golf course to where a footpath emerges onto the shore from the village of Kirksanton.*

Typical summer birds of Silecroft and environs include swift, swallow, house martin, goldfinch, greenfinch, chaffinch, song thrush, jackdaw and rook. A remnant of heath land with gorse and unimproved ground flora is situated between the caravan site and the golf course. This is worth checking for spring migrants including wheatear, whitethroat, grasshopper warbler, sedge warbler, resident stonechat, linnet and skylark. Ringed plover and oyster-catcher still nest on the shingle beach despite increasing disturbance. Below

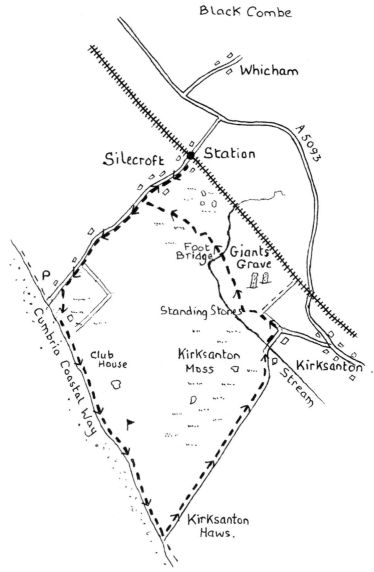

Black Combe

Whicham

A.5093

Silecroft ⁰ Station

Foot
Bridge Giant's
Grave

Standing Stones

Cumbria Coastal Way

Club
House

Kirksanton
Moss

Kirksanton
Stream

Kirksanton

Kirksanton
Haws.

the shingle bar mixed flocks of waders, gulls and terns gather on the sandy beach as the tide laps towards them and are worth scrutinising. Glaucous gull may appear in winter while on the tide-line small groups of twite and the odd snow bunting are possible. Peregrine falcon, merlin and kestrel are likely to turn up at any time hunting over the coastal fringe.

At a convenient location on the edge of the embankment stop and enjoy lunch while watching the rising tide. If your visit coincides with a good blow from the west and seasonal passage you might be here for some time doing an organised sea watch. Make yourself comfortable because sea watching demands concentration and the essential tools of the trade which are warm waterproof clothing, telescope, a tripod, binoculars, notebook and a good field guide.

During suitable weather conditions, particularly gales, a good range of passage seabirds have been recorded off the west Cumbrian coast in spring and autumn, including sooty shearwater, storm petrel, Leach's petrel, terns, Arctic, pomarine, long-tailed and great skua, fulmar, kittiwake, guillemot and razorbill. Flocks of gannets are often to be seen fishing the Irish Sea during the spring and summer months. During autumn and winter expect to see offshore flocks of common scoter, red-breasted merganser, red-throated diver, great crested grebe and wigeon. March and April brings red-throated divers drifting northwards with the odd great northern diver amongst them.

2. *Locate the wide bridleway between the southern end of Silecroft golf course and the landward sand dune complex. Indeed if you pass a wind-farm and reach a sign indicating 'Lakeland Naturist Outdoor Club,' or its naked members languishing in the sand dunes, you have gone past it so beat a hasty retreat forthwith! Any shocks might now be tempered by a therapeutic walk east along the footpath to Layrigg Farm. Thereafter pass over a stream and turn left at the first minor junction on the left to a converted farm at Standing Stones. Follow the yellow way-markers before crossing the stream over a narrow footbridge and then heading right to the left hand corner of a large field where a track leads onto a lane taking you back to Silecroft.*

Royal fern. (photo by D. Hindle)

The bridleway east from the shore follows a good old fashioned lane with high banks supporting a prolific flora, and invertebrates including many species of butterfly. Harebells, birds' foot trefoil, red campion, ragged robin and foxgloves are here in abundance and there is even a clump of Osmunda regalis – Royal Fern – perhaps symbolising Cumbria's botanical heritage. Here fledgling stonechats survey their new world from the tops of gorse bushes anxiously guarded by alarmed parents, while whitethroats scald from dense cover. Skylarks ascend into an azure sky with their seemingly unceasing melodic song above the fields of Layrigg Farm. In April countless generations of swallows return from tropical Africa to the same outbuildings after circumnavigating many hazards and the vast Sahara Desert. Beyond the farm lane and to the north east is the marshy and willow scrub area of Kirksanton Haws which is a good for roe deer, several species of warbler, reed bunting, little owl and sometimes barn owl. Barn owls have enjoyed mixed breeding success in recent years and the causes of national declines are well documented. A few years ago the ongoing threat of local barn conversions manifested itself with the immediate loss of an established breeding pair in a farm building near the 'giant's grave'.

At Standing Stones any children in the party might like to take a slight diversion to see the 'giants grave,' Follow a hedge to Standing Stones, and then double back to the building of the same name to regain the footpath to Silecroft. The megalithic stones known as the giant's grave stand at over ten feet high and despite the fabled giant these stones have dominated the Cumbrian landscape since time immemorial and were first documented in 1309. The flora and fauna will have changed quite a bit since then for alas the old coastal moss-lands and heath are a diminishing habitat throughout England.

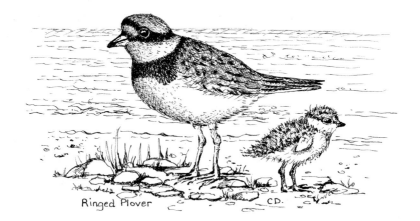

Ringed Plover   CD.

The ascent of Black Combe

skylark

Start: Start and finish at Silecroft
Grid reference: 130820
Distance: 9 km (5.6 miles)
Time: Allow 4 to 5 hours
Grade: Moderate
General: Car parking toilet and refreshment facilities at Silecroft

THIS WALK EXTENDS FROM SILECROFT to the summit of Black Combe and provides an opportunity to see a range of upland birds. For safety reasons take a compass and do not attempt to climb the Combe when there is the slightest hint of low cloud or when the local's say, 'the Combe has got a cap on it today'. In conditions of poor visibility both the view and the birds will then take a bit of finding and you might even get lost or worse! Be warned that east of the rounded summit there are rocky slopes with high crags and screes.

The isolated outcrop of Black Combe's rugged grandeur can be seen dominating the landscape from many of the walks covered by this book and represents our northern limit. It is therefore fitting to make the ascent of this lone sentinel which stands at around 600 metres high.

1. *From Silecroft Station walk inland through the village and follow the main road left towards Whicham, taking the first turning right at the road junction at the principle road junction. Walk towards Whicham Church and take the first turning left along a pictur-esque lane to the start of the climb up the south-west face of Black Combe. After passing the farm cross over a stile and follow a grassy track up through the lower slopes of the valley of Moor Gill Beck to a steep stretch before gaining the 400 metre contour. This is* *the hardest bit and from here on the pace is more relaxing before reaching a subsidiary peak and eventually an arrow of stones pointing right to the summit. The easiest and safest way down is to retrace your steps to Whicham Church.*

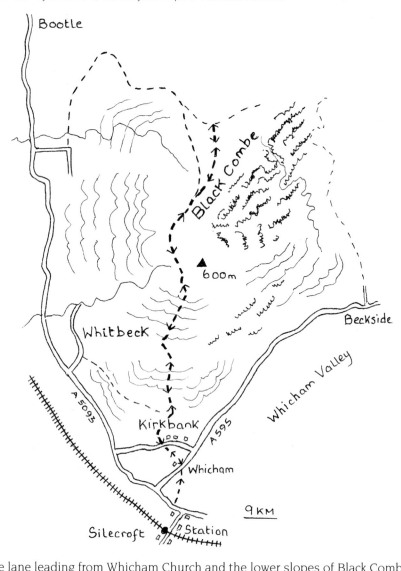

The lane leading from Whicham Church and the lower slopes of Black Combe may produce linnet, blackcap, willow warbler, long-tailed tit, goldcrest, stonechat, meadow pipit, skylark, pied wagtail and a sadly declining population of yellowhammer which unfortunately is mirrored elsewhere in northern England. The instantly recognisable call of the male cuckoo compels attention and is warmly regarded as one of the harbingers of spring. The cuckoo has sadly declined in many parts of Britain but the fells remain one of its strongholds. The male calls both in flight and when perched but despite this it is often difficult to locate. When calling from a perch he has a very characteristic pose. He bows forward, lowering the head and drooping the wings while fanning the elevated tail.

Yellowhammer, cuckoo and whinchat still haunt the lower bracken covered slopes of the combe and at higher elevations the cloughs and crags sometimes attract the ring ousel or mountain blackbird but you will be lucky to see one. However, there is one past master on song that you should hear while ascending to the summit; no prizes for getting it right but this is what Cumbrian poet and naturalist, William Wordsworth, had to say about the charismatic skylark:

> 'Up with me; Up with me into the clouds!
> For thy song, — is strong;
> Up with me; up with me into the clouds!
> Singing, singing,
> With clouds and sky about thee ringing,
> Lift me, guide, till I find,
> That spot which seems so to thy mind! [1]

Take a walk eastwards from the trig point to enjoy a panoramic view over screes and crags and Black Combe's eastern buttress of White Combe. This is an excellent place to enjoy the tranquillity of the mountain with a timely meal break. At the same time listen and look out for upland raptors, typically represented by peregrine, kestrel, buzzard and sometimes merlin. The raucous call of the raven and the familiar calls of jackdaws may often be heard in this habitat that is shared with meadow pipit and wheatear.

At the summit any lack of birds may be compensated for by the views to be enjoyed which broadly equate with the topography of the area covered by this book. To the south west the view of Blackpool Tower and the coastal plain of the Wyre estuary at Fleetwood extend north across Morecambe Bay to Walney Island, the Duddon estuary and the Lake District's western and central mountains and valleys. On a particularly clear day it may be possible to make out the mountains of North Wales, Dumfries and Galloway, the Isle of Man's Snaefell and the Irish coast.

Whinchat

---

1   *To a Skylark.* Poems of the Fancy, William Wordsworth, 10 lines 1–7

Seasonal Occurrence Chart

THIS IS INTENDED AS A GUIDE as to when species can be found throughout each month of the year. However it must be remembered that there are many variations between species, habitats and seasons, so the categories given for a particular species are subjective and are only intended as a guide. The abundance of a bird and the habitat that it occupies can change with the seasons. Birds are listed in the chart in alphabetical order of their common name. Extreme rarities are not included. The chance of seeing a species will also depend upon the experience of the observer and his knowledge of calls and song and the habitat frequented.

Key

● Only very exceptional sightings.

● A few present and unlikely to be seen.

● Present in only small numbers in suitable habitat within the area.

● Frequent and likely to be encountered in suitable habitat within the area

	Jan	Feb	Mar	Apr	May	Jun	Jul	Aug	Sep	Oct	Nov	Dec
Arctic skua				•••	••••		•••	••••	••••			
Arctic tern				•••	••••	••••	••••	••••	••••			
Avocet			•••	••••	••••	••••	••••	••••	••			
Bar-tailed godwit	••••	••••	••••	••••	•••	•••	••••	••••	••••	••••	••••	••••
Barn owl	••••	••••	••••	••••	••••	••••	••••	••••	••••	••••	••••	••••
Barnacle goose	••••	••••	•••						•••	••••	••••	••••
Bearded tit	••••	••••	••••	••••	••••	••••	••••	••••	••••	••••	••••	••••
Bewick's swan	••••	••••	•••						•••	••••	••••	••••
Bittern	••••	••••	••••	••••	••••	••••	••••	••••	••••	••••	••••	••••
Black redstart	••••	••••	•••						•••	••••	••••	••••
Black tern					••••			•••	•••			
Black-headed gull	••••	••••	••••	••••	••••	••••	••••	••••	••••	••••	••••	••••
Black-tailed godwit	••••	••••	••••	••••	•••		•••	••••	••••	••••	••••	••••
Black-throated diver	••••	••••	••••	•••					•••	••••	••••	••••
Blackcap	•••	••••	•••	••••	••••	••••	••••	••••	••••	•••	••••	••••
Blue tit	••••	••••	••••	••••	••••	••••	••••	••••	••••	••••	••••	••••
Brambling	••••	••••	••••	•••					•••	••••	••••	••••
Brent goose	••••	••••	•••						•••	••••	••••	••••
Bullfinch	••••	••••	••••	••••	••••	••••	••••	••••	••••	••••	••••	••••
Buzzard	••••	••••	••••	••••	••••	••••	••••	••••	••••	••••	••••	••••
Canada goose	••••	••••	••••	••••	••••	••••	••••	••••	••••	••••	••••	••••
Carrion crow	••••	••••	••••	••••	••••	••••	••••	••••	••••	••••	••••	••••
Chaffinch	••••	••••	••••	••••	••••	••••	••••	••••	••••	••••	••••	••••
Chiffchaff			•••	••••	••••	••••	••••	••••	••••	•••	•••	•••
Coal tit	••••	••••	••••	••••	••••	••••	••••	••••	••••	••••	••••	••••
Collared dove	••••	••••	••••	••••	••••	••••	••••	••••	••••	••••	••••	••••
Common gull	•••	••••	•••	••••	•••	•••	•••	••••	••••	••••	••••	••••
Common sandpiper			•••	••••	••••	••••	••••	••••	•••	•••		
Common scoter	••••	••••	••••	•••				•••	••••	••••	••••	••••

	Jan	Feb	Mar	Apr	May	Jun	Jul	Aug	Sep	Oct	Nov	Dec
Common tern				●	●	●	●	●	●			
Coot	●	●	●	●	●	●	●	●	●	●	●	●
Cormorant	●	●	●	●	●	●	●	●	●	●	●	●
Crossbill	●	●	●						●	●	●	●
Cuckoo				●	●	●	●	●	●			
Curlew	●	●	●	●	●	●	●	●	●	●	●	●
Curlew sandpiper				●	●		●	●	●	●		
Dipper	●	●	●	●	●	●	●	●	●	●	●	●
Dotterel				●	●			●	●			
Dunlin		●	●	●	●	●	●	●	●	●	●	●
Dunnock	●	●	●	●	●	●	●	●	●	●	●	●
Eider	●	●	●	●	●	●	●	●	●	●	●	●
Feral pigeon	●	●	●	●	●	●	●	●	●	●	●	●
Fieldfare	●	●	●	●	●			●		●	●	●
Fulmar	●	●	●	●	●	●	●	●	●	●	●	●
Gadwall	●	●	●	●	●	●	●	●	●	●	●	●
Gannet	●	●	●	●	●	●	●	●	●	●	●	●
Garden warbler				●	●	●	●	●	●			
Gargeney			●	●	●	●	●	●	●			
Glaucous gull	●	●	●						●	●	●	●
Goldcrest	●	●	●	●	●	●	●	●	●	●	●	●
Golden plover	●	●	●	●	●	●	●	●	●	●	●	●
Goldeneye	●	●	●	●	●			●		●	●	●
Goldfinch	●	●	●	●	●	●	●	●	●	●	●	●
Goosander	●	●	●	●	●	●	●	●	●	●	●	●
Goshawk	●	●	●	●	●	●	●	●	●	●	●	●
Grasshopper warbler				●	●	●	●	●	●			
Great black-backed gull	●	●	●	●	●	●	●	●	●	●	●	●
Great crested grebe	●	●	●	●	●	●	●	●	●	●	●	●

	Jan	Feb	Mar	Apr	May	Jun	Jul	Aug	Sep	Oct	Nov	Dec
Great skua					••••	••••		••••	••••			
Great spotted woodpecker	••••	••••	••••	••••	••••	••••	••••	••••	••••	••••	••••	••••
Great tit	••••	••••	••••	••••	••••	••••	••••	••••	••••	••••	••••	••••
Green sandpiper	••••	••••	••••	••••	••••		••••	••••	••••	••••	••••	••••
Green woodpecker	••••	••••	••••	••••	••••	••••	••••	••••	••••	••••	••••	••••
Greenfinch	••••	••••	••••	••••	••••	••••	••••	••••	••••	••••	••••	••••
Greenshank	••••	••••	••••	••••	••••	••••	••••	••••	••••	••••	••••	••••
Grey heron	••••	••••	••••	••••	••••	••••	••••	••••	••••	••••	••••	••••
Grey partridge	••••	••••	••••	••••	••••	••••	••••	••••	••••	••••	••••	••••
Grey plover	••••	••••	••••	••••	••••	••••	••••	••••	••••	••••	••••	••••
Grey wagtail	••••	••••	••••	••••	••••	••••	••••	••••	••••	••••	••••	••••
Greylag goose	••••	••••	••••	••••	••••	••••	••••	••••	••••	••••	••••	••••
Guillemot	••••	••••	••••	••••	••••	••••	••••	••••	••••	••••	••••	••••
Hawfinch	••••	••••	••••	••••	••••	••••	••••	••••	••••	••••	••••	••••
Hen harrier		••••	••••	••••	••••	••••	••••	••••	••••	••••	••••	••••
Herring gull	••••	••••	••••	••••	••••	••••	••••	••••	••••	••••	••••	••••
Hobby					••••	••••	••••	••••				
House martin				••••	••••	••••	••••	••••	••••	•••		
House sparrow	••••	••••	••••	••••	••••	••••	••••	••••	••••	••••	••••	••••
Iceland gull	••••	••••									••••	••••
Jack snipe	••••	••••	••••	••••					••••	••••	••••	••••
Jackdaw	••••	••••	••••	••••	••••	••••	••••	••••	••••	••••	••••	••••
Jay	••••	••••	••••	••••	••••	••••	••••	••••	••••	••••	••••	••••
Kestrel	••••	••••	••••	••••	••••	••••	••••	••••	••••	••••	••••	••••
Kingfisher	••••	••••	••••	••••	••••	••••	••••	••••	••••	••••	••••	••••
Kittiwake	••••	••••	••••	••••	••••	••••	••••	••••	••••	••••	••••	••••
Knot	••••	••••	••••	••••	••••	••••	••••	••••	••••	••••	••••	••••
Lapwing	••••	••••	••••	••••	••••	••••	••••	••••	••••	••••	••••	••••
Leach's petrel								••••	••••	••••		

	Jan	Feb	Mar	Apr	May	Jun	Jul	Aug	Sep	Oct	Nov	Dec
Lesser black-backed gull	••••	••••	••••	••••	••••	••••	••••	••••	••••	••••	••••	••••
Lesser spotted woodpecker	••••	••••	••••	••••	••••	••••	••••	••••	••••	••••	••••	••••
Lesser whitethroat				•••	••••	••••	••••	••••	••••			
Linnet	••••	••••	••••	••••	••••	••••	••••	••••	••••	••••	••••	••••
Little egret	••••	••••	••••	••••	••••	••••	••••	••••	••••	••••	••••	••••
Little grebe	••••	••••	••••	••••	••••	••••	••••	••••	••••	••••	••••	••••
Little gull	••••	••••	••••	•••••	••••	••••	••••	••••	••••	••••	••••	••••
Little owl	••••	••••	••••	••••	••••	••••	••••	••••	••••	••••	••••	••••
Little ringed plover				••••	••••	••••	••••	••••	••••			
Little stint					••••	••••		••••	••••	••••		
Little tern				••••	••••		••••	••••	••••			
Long-eared owl	••••	••••	••••	••••	••••	••••	••••	••••	••••	••••	••••	••••
Long-tailed tit	••••	••••	••••	••••	••••	••••	••••	••••	••••	••••	••••	••••
Mallard	••••	••••	••••	••••	••••	••••	••••	••••	••••	••••	••••	••••
Manx shearwater				••••	••••	••••	••••	••••	••			
Marsh harrier				••••	••••	••••	••••	••••	••			
Marsh tit	••••	••••	••••	••••	••••	••••	••••	••••	••••	••••	••••	••••
Meadow pipit	••••	••••	••••	••••	••••	••••	••••	••••	••••	••••	••••	••••
Mediterranean gull	••••	••••	••••	••••	••••	••••	••••	••••	••••	••••	••••	••••
Merlin	••••	••••	••••	••••	••••	••••	••••	••••	••••	••••	••••	••••
Mistle thrush	••••	••••	••••	••••	••••	••••	••••	••••	••••	••••	••••	••••
Moorhen	••••	••••	••••	••••	••••	••••	••••	••••	••••	••••	••••	••••
Mute swan	••••	••••	••••	••••	••••	••••	••••	••••	••••	••••	••••	••••
Nuthatch	••••	••••	••••	••••	••••	••••	••••	••••	••••	••••	••••	••••
Osprey			••••	••••	••••	••••	••••	••••	••••			
Oystercatcher	••••	••••	••••	••••	••••	••••	••••	••••	••••	••••	••••	••••
Peregrine	••••	••••	••••	••••	••••	••••	••••	••••	••••	••••	••••	••••
Pheasant	••••	••••	••••	••••	••••	••••	••••	••••	••••	••••	••••	••••
Pied flycatcher				••••	••••	••••	••••	••••	••••			

	Jan	Feb	Mar	Apr	May	Jun	Jul	Aug	Sep	Oct	Nov	Dec
Pied wagtail	••••	••••	••••	••••	••••	••••	••••	••••	••••	••••	••••	••••
Pink-footed goose	••••	••••	••••	••••	····	····	····	····	••••	••••	••••	••••
Pintail	••••	••••	••••	••••	•••		····	····	••••	••••	••••	••••
Pochard	••••	••••	••••	••••	••••	••••	••••	••••	••••	••••	••••	••••
Pomarine skua						••••			••••	••••		
Raven	••••	••••	••••	••••	••••	••••	••••	••••	••••	••••	••••	••••
Razorbill	····	····	····	····	····						····	····
Red grouse	••••	••••	••••	••••	••••	••••	••••	••••	••••	••••	••••	••••
Red-breasted merganser	••••	••••	••••	••••	••••	••••	••••	••••	••••	••••	••••	••••
Red-legged partridge	••••	••••	••••	••••	••••	••••	••••	••••	••••	••••	••••	••••
Red-throated diver	····	····	····	····					····	····	····	····
Redpoll	••••	••••	••••	••••	••••	••••	••••	••••	••••	••••	••••	••••
Red kite	····	····	····	····	····	····	····	····	····	····	····	····
Redshank	••••	••••	••••	••••	••••	••••	••••	••••	••••	••••	••••	••••
Redstart				···•	••••	••••	••••	••••	····			
Redwing	••••	••••	••••	••••	····				···•	••••	••••	••••
Reed bunting	••••	••••	••••	••••	••••	••••	••••	••••	••••	••••	••••	••••
Reed warbler			···•	••••	••••	••••	••••	••••	···•	•		
Ring ouzel			···•	••••	••••	••••	••••	••••	····	····		
Ringed plover	••••	••••	••••	••••	••••	••••	••••	••••	••••	••••	••••	••••
Robin	••••	••••	••••	••••	••••	••••	••••	••••	••••	••••	••••	••••
Rock pipit	····	····	····	····						····	····	····
Rook	••••	••••	••••	••••	••••	••••	••••	••••	••••	••••	••••	••••
Ruddy duck	••••	••••	••••	••••	••••	••••	••••	••••	••••	••••	••••	••••
Ruff			····	••••	••••		····	••••	····			
Sand martin			··••	••••	••••	••••	••••	••••	•···			
Sanderling	••••	••••	••••	••••	····		····	••••	••••	••••	••••	••••
Sandwich tern			···•	••••	••••	••••	••••	••••	••			
Scaup	····	····	··							····	••••	••••

	Jan	Feb	Mar	Apr	May	Jun	Jul	Aug	Sep	Oct	Nov	Dec
Sedge warbler				••••	••••	••••	••••	••••	••••			
Shag		••••	••••	••••	••••			••••	••••	••••	••••	••••
Shelduck	••••	••••	••••	••••	••••	••••	••••	••••	••••	••••	••••	••••
Short-eared owl	••••	••••	••••	••••	••••	••••	••••	••••	••••	••••	••••	••••
Shoveler	••••	••••	••••	••••	••••	••••	••••	••••	••••	••••	••••	••••
Siskin	••••	••••	••••	••••	••••	••••	••••	••••	••••	••••	••••	••••
Skylark	••••	••••	••••	••••	••••	••••	••••	••••	••••	••••	••••	••••
Slavonian grebe	••••	••••	••••							••••	••••	••••
Snipe	••••	••••	••••	••••	••••	••••	••••	••••	••••	••••	••••	••••
Snow bunting	••••	••••	••••							••••	••••	••••
Song thrush	••••	••••	••••	••••	••••	••••	••••	••••	••••	••••	••••	••••
Smew	••••	••••									••••	••••
Sparrowhawk	••••	••••	••••	••••	••••	••••	••••	••••	••••	••••	••••	••••
Spoonbill				••••	••••	••••	••••	••••	••			
Spotted flycatcher				••••	••••	••••	••••	••••	••••			
Spotted redshank	••••	••••	••••	••••	••••	••••	••••	••••	••••	••••	••••	••••
Stock dove	••••	••••	••••	••••	••••	••••	••••	••••	••••	••••	••••	••••
Stonechat	••••	••••	••••	••••	••••	••••	••••	••••	••••	••••	••••	••••
Storm petrel					••••		••••	••••	••••	••••		
Swallow			••••	••••	••••	••••	••••	••••	••••	••••	••••	
Swift				••••	••••	••••	••••	••••	••			
Tawny owl	••••	••••	••••	••••	••••	••••	••••	••••	••••	••••	••••	••••
Teal	••••	••••	••••	••••	••••	••••	••••	••••	••••	••••	••••	••••
Tree pipit				••••	••••	••••	••••	••••	••••	••••		
Tree sparrow	••••	••••	••••	••••	••••	••••	••••	••••	••••	••••	••••	••••
Treecreeper	••••	••••	••••	••••	••••	••••	••••	••••	••••	••••	••••	••••
Tufted duck	••••	••••	••••	••••	••••	••••	••••	••••	••••	••••	••••	••••
Turnstone	••••	••••	••••	••••	••••	••••	••••	••••	••••	••••	••••	••••
Twite	••••	••••	••••	••••	••••	••••	••••	••••	••••	••••	••••	••••

	Jan	Feb	Mar	Apr	May	Jun	Jul	Aug	Sep	Oct	Nov	Dec
Water pipit	••••	••••	••••							••••	••••	••••
Water rail	••••	••••	••••	••••	••••	••••	••••	••••	••••	••••	••••	••••
Waxwing	••••	••••	••••							••••	••••	••••
Wheatear			••••	••••	••••	••••	••••	••••	••••	••••		
Whimbrel				••••	•••			••••	••••	••••		
Whinchat				••••	••••	••••	••••	••••	••••	••••		
Whitethroat				••••	••••	••••	••••	••••	••••			
White-fronted goose	••••	••••	••••	•						••••	••••	••••
Whooper swan	••••	••••	••••	••••	••••	••••	••••	••••	••••	••••	••••	••••
Wigeon	••••	••••	••••	••••	••••	••••	••••	••••	••••	••••	••••	••••
Willow warbler				••••	••••	••••	••••	••••	••••			
Wood sandpiper				••••				••••	••••			
Wood warbler				••••	••••	••••	••••	••••				
Woodcock	••••	••••	••••	••••	••••	••••	••••	••••	••••	••••	••••	••••
Wren	••••	••••	••••	••••	••••	••••	••••	••••	••••	••••	••••	••••
Yellow wagtail				••••	••••	••••	••••	••••	••••			
Yellow hammer	••••	••••	••••	••••	••••	••••	••••	••••	••••	••••	••••	••••